Melinda+ Dale Howard

MW01094757

LEFT BANK

#2

extinction

BLUE HERON PUBLISHING, INC.
HILLSBORO, OREGON

Editor: Linny Stovall
Associate Editor: Stephen J. Beard
Publisher: Dennis Stovall
Staff: Mary Jo Schimelpfenig, Christian Seapy, William Woodall
Advertising: John Johnson
Interior Design: Dennis Stovall
Cover Design: Marcia Barrentine
Advisors: Ann Chandonnet, Madeline DeFrees, Katherine Dunn, Jim Hepworth,
    Ursula Le Guin, Lynda Sexson, J.T. Stewart, Alan Twigg, Shawn Wong

Editorial correspondence: Linny Stovall or Stephen Beard, Left Bank, Blue Heron
Publishing, Inc., 24450 N.W. Hansen Road, Hillsboro, OR 97124. Submissions are
welcome if accompanied by a stamped, self-addressed envelope. Otherwise they will
not be returned. Authors must have a strong connection to the Pacific Northwest.
Editorial guidelines are available on request (include SASE).

Left Bank, a magazine in book form, is published semiannually by Blue Heron Publishing, Inc., 24450 N.W. Hansen Road, Hillsboro, OR 97124. Subscriptions are
$14 per year (postage included). Single issues are $7.95 (plus $1.50 s&h). Left Bank
is distributed to the book trade and libraries in the United States by Consortium
Book Sales and Distribution, 287 East Sixth Street, Suite 365, Saint Paul, MN
55101. In Canada, Left Bank is available through Milestone Publications Ltd., PO
Box 35548, Stn. E, Vancouver, B.C. V6M 4G8.

Rights & permissions: "Love And Boundaries," Jerome Gold, previously appeared in
two now defunct journals, *The Next War* and *Itchy Planet*. § "Euclid's Hell," Robert
Heilman, appeared in a slightly different form in the August 1991 issue of *The Sun*,
published in Chapel Hill, North Carolina. § "Apologia," Barry Lopez, appeared origi-
nally in *Witness* and later in *Harper's* and is reprinted by permission of Sterling Lord
Literistic, Inc. § "A Future As Big As Indonesia," first printed in *Outside* magazine,
July 1991, is reprinted with permission of David Quammen. All rights reserved.
Copyright © 1991 by David Quammen.

Cover and inside art: "Ocumicho" by Jack McLarty

LEFT BANK #2, Summer 1992
Copyright © 1992 by Blue Heron Publishing, Inc.

ISBN 0-036085-50-9
ISSN 1056-7429

CONTENTS

Introduction

Earlier this year, a series of hearings — in effect a trial — was held in nearby Portland, Oregon. At question was the fate of *Strix occidentalis caurina*, a woodland creature so naive about the international demand for timber that it insists on living in mature Western forests prized for the two by fours and plywood into which their trees can be converted.

On one side of the hearings was the Fish and Wildlife Service. On the other side was the Bureau of Land Management. Each side's attorneys offered exhibits; called, questioned and cross-examined witnesses; demanded rulings about the admissibility of certain evidence.

Science was considered and questioned, as were certain legal niceties revolving around the issues of who was supposed to do what and when.

The political assertions of those supporting both sides were aired in the press with the usual inflamed rhetoric shedding much more temperature than illumination.

The claims and declamations, together with less formal pleas from a non-refereed forum following the official proceedings, were to be compiled, collated, bound and presented to the Endangered Species Committee, a collection of federal pooh-bahs unofficially known as the God Squad. The committee has, in essence, the power to turn thumbs up or thumbs down on the recommendations of eminent scientists, many of whom have studied the issue for years, that certain habitat in Oregon's remaining old-growth forests be reserved to assure the survival of *S. occidentalis*, also known as the northern spotted owl.

We can't say how the God Squad will rule; we only note that spotted owls were not able to testify. Given the bitterness and cynicism of the proceedings, we suspect they would have been ruled out of order had they been capable of speaking. We are left to wonder what they might have said.

In place of their testimony, all we can offer is *Left Bank #2: Extinction,* in which we examine the fate of creatures, nations, and worlds through the sharpest lenses of literature.

We invite you to read. And to draw what lessons you may.

— The Editors

Foreword

Thoughts on Extinction

by David T. Suzuki

Contrary to the popular image of people sprinkled sparsely across a vast landscape, most Canadians do not live near wilderness or on farms. Eighty percent of us live in cities and towns which tend to cling to the border with the US. The propensity for city living is similar in the US. Urban dwellers in a human-created environment find it easy to accept the illusion that we have escaped our biological roots and now master our destiny by the control and manipulation of our surroundings. Our schism from the rest of nature is at the heart of the global ecocrisis.

Human beings are "animals." This is a biological fact but when stated, invites immediate and heated dispute. We reinforce the notion of our superiority to other beings by the pejorative use of words like "chicken," "pig," "jackass," "worm," "ape" or "snake." We are so disconnected from the natural world that sustains us that many children are unaware that every bit of our food was once a living plant or animal. The ecological implications of the origin of our water and electricity and the destiny of our sewers and garbage are not appreciated by most urban citizens.

We are even buffered from death, the one indisputable and inescapable fact of living that reminds us of our biology. Death has become unfamiliar, a process managed in hospitals by professionals — doctors, nurses, chaplains, lawyers and undertakers. Today aging and death are often referred to as "diseases" as if they are defects that can be treated by medical forces and conquered by scientists.

But death is an integral part of living that ensures the long term survival of species and communities of organisms. Each new generation of life receives a gift of the flesh and protoplasm of others in an unbroken ribbon back to the first primordial cell and ahead to every future being. This struck me forcefully on my first trip above the Arctic circle when I came across the skeleton of a muskox that had lain there for years. For a meter around it, a veritable oasis of miniature flowers bloomed, sustained by the weak broth of nutrients still leaching from those bones in that unforgiving environment.

The pain of our knowledge that death is the inevitable consequence of life is somehow softened by the recognition that we are the earth through the plants and animals we consume, we are the rains and oceans that flow through our veins, and we are the breath of the forests of the land and all green things of the sea. And so long as life goes on, we will persist as a part of it.

Seen in this context, extinction is also a natural part of life. If 99% of all species that have ever lived are now extinct, they passed away at the rate of perhaps a species every year or two. On a planet with tens of millions of species, their disappearance wouldn't have been noticeable.

Episodes of mass extinctions have punctuated life's record in the past, the most notorious being the disappearance of dinosaurs. But our species may be unique as the perpetrator, both unwitting and deliberate, of rapid, multiple extermination. Paleolithic people squirting across the Bering bridge may have been the cause of an extinction front of large mammals that accompanied their passage down North and then South America. And in more recent times, human occupation of Australia, Madagascar, New Zealand and Hawaii was followed by a wave of species extinction.

But modern industrial *Homo sapiens* has acquired unprecedented numbers and technological musclepower that are now altering the biosphere itself. Whole communities are wiped out almost overnight by immense dams, giant clearcuts, agriculture, and development. And the scale and novelty of the detritus of industrial activity is altering the very support systems of all life — air, water, soil and biodiversity — that are responsible for the cleansing, regeneration and productivity of the layer of protoplasm that carpets the Earth.

Human beings take pride in the possession of intelligence yet seem unable to do what our earliest forebearers did — create a future and choose from options to assure our survival. We boast of loving our children yet act in ways that guarantee their lives will be far more restricted and burdened with the cost of our profligate ways. We must reimmerse ourselves into the web of living things who are our kin and sustain us.

EXTINCTION

Euclid's Hell

by Robert Heilman

During the Watergate summer of 1973, while Sam Ervin roasted Nixon administration witnesses, I worked as a roofer on a housing development in New Mexico. The days had an amazing sameness. The one hundred degree-plus weather held for weeks on end. Though there were six different floor plans for the housing units that we were building, they had only two roof styles — one with a skylight in front and one without. The shingles were either light or dark brown. Each roof took two days to lay. Every measurement, every vent, and each piece of metal flashing was the same as the roof before and the roof that followed. The gravel-coated asphalt shingles formed a Euclidean hell more arid and featureless than the surrounding desert.

Every day a certain cloud would form over the same peak of the San Juan range in the distance. When it grew to the right size, I would confirm with my pocketwatch what the cloud had already told me: lunch time was at hand.

In the relative coolness beneath the roof we ate our meal with the assembled hardtimers, hippies, Chicanos and Indians who made up the construction crews and listened as the contractors argued. There were frequent arguments, sparked by trade chauvinism, conflicting schedules and methedrine.

One day the head electrician and the framing foreman got into it. The electrician drew out the blueprints for the house and pointed from the plans to the wall and back again saying: "See? It calls for a doubled stud right here. How the hell can I hang a box here unless you double it up?"

The carpenter was nonplussed. "This place was screwed-up from the get. The foundation's off; the slab's wrong. Face it: it wasn't built to the plan — it was built to the hill. You've got to make allowances."

11

Despite the fact that the carpenter really should have doubled-up that stud. I remember feeling that there was something important about the exchange without understanding its significance. Like a Sufi story, the carpenter's complaint came back to me over the years, always ringing true, but only slowly revealing its implications.

It was, I believe, the ancient conflict between what is and what ought to be, between the vision and the reality, between mind and matter, with mind stubbornly insisting that its expectations be met and reality even more obstinately refusing to be something it isn't. "Wish in one hand and shit in the other — see which one fills up first," goes the proverb.

We were, as craftsmen, caught up in a no-win situation. Someone, or some group of somebodies, somewhere, had created a plan, a vision set forth on paper, as clean and abstract as a problem in geometry. A housing tract, consisting of housing units, would rise on some lots. Every detail had been considered beforehand. It simply remained for us to follow the dictates of blue lines on white paper.

And yet, that paper village could never stand on this earth. Nature, both human nature and Mother Nature, insured that. Stubborn reality refused to conform to the unreal desires of mind. Each piece of the plan, when put into execution, asserted its own individuality against the mind that treated it as undifferentiated, interchangeable parts. No two houses could really be the same. No two nails, of the kegs we pounded, were identical; no two boards or shingles or grains of sand in the concrete were truly the same as any other that ever was or would be. A common everyday miracle prevented, once again, the drabness of human thought from reproducing itself. Walt Whitman would have been pleased.

It's amazing to me how little respect most people seem to have for reality. The mind is a wonderful thing and perhaps most wonderfully of all, capable of tricking us into accepting its version of what takes place around us. We mistake our perceptions for the stuff of existence, repeatedly, even when we know better. Like a kitten trying to touch its image in a mirror, we reach out to the world we think we see, only to find that it's not really there.

I know many people who are terrified by the notion that reality is, by its nature, incomprehensible. A very few are delighted by it. Most people, it seems, never take up the question at all.

I have heard and read about some of the reasons that so many of us trust our perceptions more than we trust the world as it is. It's difficult to sort them all out and get a clear picture, but it's not hard to see the results.

In the spring of 1980 I was finishing up my fifth winter as a tree planter in southern Oregon. It was my sixth crew in five seasons and by that spring I'd planted 150,000 seedling trees, enough to replant something close to three hundred acres of logged off mountain slopes. At ten planters to a crew I must have helped reforest about 3,000 acres, all within an eighty mile radius of my home.

One morning we were planting some freshly clearcut land up Buck Creek, a three hundred acre rocky, ravaged reforestation unit. Our crew was attempting to plant Douglas fir seedlings with ten inch roots in a perfect eight foot by eight foot grid pattern in shallow, eroded soil and logging debris.

Over and over again, we bent our backs and swung our hoedags only to clink against rock covered with three or four inches of topsoil. We did what we could for the land, finding small pockets of soil built up on the backside of the huge, sap oozing stumps of the forest that used to be and scratching holes in the shallow spots as proof that we'd been there and found the spot unplantable.

"Shit!" someone spat after yet another arm jarring clink, "I feel like a goddamn chicken scratchin' around out here."

"Buck-buck-buh-gawk! Buck-buck-buck-buck-buh-gawk!" I answered, and the crew took up the call.

It was spring, a beautiful, sweet smelling sunny day and a sort of madness, compounded of ten wiry bodies in motion, sunshine, and the frustration of the work, overcame us. We glanced over our shoulders slyly, challenging Jack, the foreman, to stop our clucking insurrection.

Jack surveyed the scene from his stump top roost, leaning against his inspector's shovel. He lifted his hard hat, scratched his head and decided to try to change the subject. As was his wont, he spoke of the wonders of modern forestry.

"Boy they sure did a nice job on this unit. Lots of reprod." He gestured toward some scraggly residual trees. "The loggers sure pissed and moaned when we made 'em get good suspension but those naturals will really take off now that we let the sunlight in. In the old days we wouldn't have bothered, you know. Hell, ten years from now this'll all be thick as dog hair with young firs."

"Fuck-fuck-fuck-fuck-off!" someone down the line called out amid the clucking and chinking. Jack pretended he hadn't heard.

I thought of the hardscrabble canyons of Rock Creek, of the old units logged twenty and thirty years ago that we'd replanted all winter long, trying for the fifth or sixth time to bring back the forest on land whose soil had been muddying the river for decades. Something sad and ugly rose within me. I stood up, leaning on my hoedag to straighten my sore back, hitched up my tree bags to ease the chafing on my hips and turned to face my foreman.

"You're nuts." I told him, "This is totally fucking insane." I gestured downstream at the silted creek bed, at the place where we'd found chips of jasper knapped from tool cores by the Indians, at the stark grey face of Buck Rock gleaming in the sunlight for the first time in ten thousand years, at the yarder tower roaring its diesel roar and hooting like an owl as it dragged a turn of logs uphill to the waiting log trucks.

"Look at this place Jack. This ain't a forest — it's a fucking disaster. Get your head out of your ass and look at it. A hundred years from now people will wonder how the hell we could have been so fucking stupid."

The clucking had stopped. The rest of the crew stood still, grinning and watching and waiting to hear Jack's reply.

"This is good ground. This unit will come back just fine. We've done a good job logging it, the best anybody can do, with all the best techniques we've got and it'll come back just fine."

It was time to back off. I knew that. It was one thing to bait the man as a joke but challenging his profession was stepping over the line. I couldn't back off though. The accumulated poison of five winters of tree planting had turned to venom.

"Bullshit. You're fucking crazy. All you company foresters are insane. Just look at this place Jack. Take a look around you and see what's really going on here. It's totally fucking insane."

"Look, Heilman, don't fuck with me. I run a good crew and we do good work. What do you know anyway? Huh? I've got a masters degree in forestry — I know what I'm talking about. You don't know shit." he said, as if mountains were blackboards.

I'd blown my winter's job, his tone said. I thought of November and the uncertainty of finding another crew to work on. In the ten years since dropping out of high school I'd been laid off, fired from or quit thirty different jobs.

"Yeah, what do I know? I'm just a dumb-ass tree planter."

"Shut up and get back to work."

I glanced at the last seedling I'd planted, chose a likely spot eight feet away for the next one, took two steps and swung my hoedag. Up and down the line the laughter and clucking had died and the only sounds were the scraping and clinking of hoedags on rock and the distant roar of the yarder.

Jack wasn't a bad guy to work for at all. In fact, I liked him and respected him a good deal. It's not easy to ride herd on a bunch of mud-spattered brush apes and he did it well. But like a lot of nice people, he'd bought into a plan, some words on paper which he never questioned despite the evidence all around him. In his view, the plan itself was foolproof. If anything went wrong it had to be because the plan hadn't been executed properly. It never occurred to him that no plan, no matter how detailed, could ever encompass something as complex and miraculous as a mountain slope.

The lack of respect for the fact of individuality makes all sorts of horrors and cruelties not only possible, but seemingly desirable. After all, if the universe is composed of interchangeable pieces, the annihilation or impoverishment or demeaning of any one piece, whether a rock or a mountain, a tree or a forest, a person or a people, a valley or a planet, cannot have much importance.

The illusion of sameness creates a devalued currency in our language, thoughts, and emotions. We forget that the word only stands for the thing suggested, and the object itself is, by its essential nature, unknowable mystery and sacred in and of itself — simply by being.

Uniformity is a convenient fiction, useful for fooling ourselves but useless for seeing things as they really are. Never trust anyone who believes in the reality of units. They have sold their share in living for counterfeit coinage.

Apologia

by Barry Lopez

A few miles east of home in the Cascades I slow down and pull over for two raccoons, sprawled still as stones in the road. I carry them to the side and lay them in the sun-shot, windblown grass in the barrow pit. In eastern Oregon, along U.S. 20, black-tailed jackrabbits lie like welts of sod — three, four, then a fifth. By the bridge of Jordan Creek, just shy of the Idaho border, in the drainage of the Owyhee River, a crumpled adolescent porcupine leers up almost manically over its blood-flecked teeth. I carry each one away from the tarmac into a cover of grass or brush out of decency, I think. And worry. Who are these animals, their lights gone out? What journeys have fallen apart here?

I do not stop to remove each dark blister from the road. I wince before the recently dead, feel my lips tighten, see something else, a fence post, in the spontaneous aversion of my eyes, and pull over. I imagine white silk threads of life still vibrating inside them, even if the body's husk is stretched out for yards, stuck like oiled muslin to the road. The energy that held them erect leaves like a bullet; but the memory of that energy fades slowly from the wrinkled cornea, the bloodless fur.

The raccoons and, later, a red fox carry like sacks of wet gravel and sand. Each animal is like a solitary child's shoe in the road.

Once a man asked, Why do you bother? You never know, I said. The ones you give some semblance of burial, to whom you offer an apology, may have been like seers in a parallel culture. It is an act of respect, a technique of awareness.

In Idaho I hit a young sage sparrow — *thwack* against the right fender in the very split second I see it. Its companion rises a foot higher from the same spot, slow as smoke, and sails off clean into the desert. I rest the walloped bird in my left hand, my right thumb pressed to its chest. I feel for the wail of the heart. Its eyes glisten like rain on crystal. Nothing but warmth. I shut the tiny eyelids and lay it beside a clump of bunchgrass. Beyond a barbed-wire fence the overgrazed range is littered with cow flops. The road curves away to the south. I nod before I go, a ridiculous gesture, out of simple grief.

I pass four spotted skunks. The swirling air is acrid with the rupture of each life.

Darkness rises in the valleys of Idaho. East of Grand View, south of the Snake River, nighthawks swoop the road for gnats, silent on the wing as owls. On a descending curve I see two of them lying soft as clouds in the road. I turn around and come back. The sudden slowing down and my K-turn at the bottom of the hill draw the attention of a man who steps away from a tractor, a dozen yards from where the birds lie. I can tell by his step, the suspicious tilt of his head, that he is wary, vaguely proprietary. Offended, or irritated, he may throw the birds back into the road when I leave. So I wait, subdued like a penitent, a body in each hand.

He speaks first, a low voice, a deep murmur weighted with awe. He has been watching these flocks feeding just above the road for several evenings. He calls them whippoorwills. He gestures for a carcass. How odd, yes, the way they concentrate their hunting right on the road, I say. He runs a finger down the smooth arc of the belly and remarks on the small whiskered bill. He pulls one long wing out straight, but not roughly. He marvels. He glances at my car, baffled by this out-of-state courtesy. Two dozen nighthawks career past, back and forth at arm's length, feeding at our height and lower. He asks if I would mind — as though I owned it — if he took the bird up to the house to show his wife. "She's never seen anything like this." He's fascinated. "Not close."

I trust, later, he will put it in the fields, not throw the body in the trash, a whirligig.

North of Pinedale in western Wyoming on U.S. 189, below the Gros Ventre Range, I see a big doe from a great distance, the low rays of first light gleaming in her tawny reddish hair. She rests askew, like a crushed tree. I drag her to the shoulder, then down a long slope by the petals of her ears. A gunnysack of plaster mud, ears cold as rain gutters. All of her doesn't come. I climb back for the missing leg. The stains go north and off to the south as far as I can see.

On an afternoon trafficless, quiet as a cloister, headed across South Pass in the Wind River Range, I swerve violently but hit an animal, and then try to wrestle the gravel-spewing skid in a straight line along the lip of an embankment. I know even as I struggle for control the irony of this: I could pitch off here to my own death, easily. The bird is dead somewhere in the road behind me. Only a few seconds and I am safely back on the road, nauseous, light-headed.

It is hard to distinguish among younger gulls. I turn this one around slowly in my hands. It could be a western gull, a mew gull, a California gull. I do not remember well enough the bill markings, the color of the legs. I have not doubt about the vertebrae shattered beneath the seamless white of its ropy neck.

East of Lusk, Wyoming, in Nebraska, I stop for a badger. I squat on the macadam to admire the long claws, the perfect set of its teeth in the broken jaw, the ramulose shading of its fur — how it differs slightly, as does every badger's, from the drawings and pictures in the field guides. A car drifts toward us over the prairie, coming on in the other lane, a white 1962 Chevrolet station wagon. The driver slows to pass. In the bright sunlight I can't see his face, only an arm and the gesture of his thick left hand. It opens in a kind of shrug, hangs briefly in limp sadness, then extends itself in supplication. Gone past, it curls itself against the car door and is still.

Farther on in western Nebraska I pick up the small bodies of mice and birds. While I wait to retrieve these creatures I do not meet the eyes of passing drivers. Whoever they are, I feel anger toward them, in spite of the sparrow and the gull I myself have killed. We treat the attrition of lives on the road like the attrition of lives in war: horrifying, unavoidable, justified. Accepting the slaughter leaves people momentarily fractious, embarrassed. South of Broken Bow, at dawn, I cannot avoid an immature barn swallow. It hangs by its head, motionless in the slats of the grill.

I stop for a rabbit on Nebraska 806 and find, only a few feet away, a garter snake. What else have I missed, too small, too narrow? What has gone under or past me while I stared at mountains, hay meadows, fencerows, the beryl surface of rivers? In Wyoming I could not help but see pronghorn antelope swollen big as barrels by the side of the road, their legs splayed rigidly aloft. For animals that large people will stop. But how many have this habit of clearing the road of smaller creatures, people who would remove the ones that I miss? I do not imagine I am alone. As much sorrow as the man's hand conveyed in Nebraska, it meant gratitude too for burying the dead.

Still, I do not wish to meet anyone's eyes.

In southwestern Iowa, outside Clarinda, I haul a deer into high grass out of sight of the road and begin to examine it. It is still whole, but the destruction is breathtaking. The skull, I soon discover, is fractured in four places; the jaw, hanging by shreds of mandibular muscle, is broken at the symphysis, beneath the incisors. The pelvis is crushed, the left hind leg unsocketed. All but two ribs are dislocated along the vertebral column, which is complexly fractured. The intestines have been driven forward into the chest. The heart and lungs have ruptured the chest wall at the base of the neck. The signature of a tractor-trailer truck: 78,000 pounds at 65 mph.

In front of a motel room in Ottumwa I fingerscrape the dry stiff carcasses of bumblebees, wasps, and butterflies from the grill and headlight mountings, and I scrub with a wet cloth to soften and wipe away the nap of crumbles, the insects, the aerial plankton of spiders and mites. I am uneasy carrying so many of the dead. The carnage is so obvious.

In Illinois, west of Kankakee, two raccoons as young as the ones in Oregon. In Indiana another raccoon, a gray squirrel. When I make the left turn into the driveway at the house of a friend outside of South Bend, it is evening, hot and muggy. I can hear cicadas in a lone elm. I'm glad to be here.

From the driveway entrance I look back down Indiana 23, toward Indiana 8, remembering the farm roads of Illinois and Iowa. I remember how beautiful it was in the limpid air to drive Nebraska 2 through the Sand Hills, to see how far at dusk the land was etched east and west of Wyoming 28. I remember the imposition of the Wind River Mountains in a hard, blue sky beneath white ranks of buttonhook clouds, windy hayfields on the Snake River Plain, the welcome of Russian olive trees and willows in creek bottoms. The transformation of the heart such beauty engenders is not enough tonight to let me shed the heavier memory, a catalogue too morbid to write out, to vivid to ignore.

I stand in the driveway now, listening to the cicadas whirring in the dark tree. My hands grip the sill of the open window at the driver's side, and I lean down as if to speak to someone still sitting there. The weight I wish to fall I cannot fathom, a sorrow over the world's dark hunger.

A light comes on over the porch. I hear a dead bolt thrown, the shiver of a door pulled free. The word of atonement I pronounce are too inept to offer me release. Or forgiveness. My friend is floating across the tree-shadowed lawn. What is to be done with the desire for exculpation?

"Later than we thought you'd be," he says.

I do not want the lavabo. I wish to make amends.

"I made more stops than I thought I would," I answer.

"Well, bring this in. And whatever I can take," he says.

I anticipate, in the powerful antidote of our conversation, the reassurance of a human enterprise, the forgiving embrace of the rational. It waits within, beyond the slow tail-wagging of two dogs standing at the screen door.

Forks

by Sallie Tisdale

When the French-Canadian Paul Bunyan moved to the United States, he and his blue ox Babe became "Real Americans." Real Americans, Paul knew, were hard workers, looking for opportunity. In the midst of his joy at his newfound citizenship, he sought direction.

"A whisper stirred in his heart: 'To work! Take advantage of your opportunity!' The whisper got louder and more insistent every moment; and at last the idea it spoke possessed Paul Bunyan, and he sat down to ponder it, letting Babe graze and roll on the clover-covered hills.

"Now the whisper became an insistent cry: 'Work! Work! Work!' Paul Bunyan looked up, and he seemed to see the word shining among the clouds; he looked down then into the vast valley, and he seemed to see — by the holy old mackinaw! he did see — the forest of his second dream! And now he knew it: his Life Work was to begin here.

"Real America was covered with forests. A forest was composed of trees. A felled and trimmed tree was a log. Paul Bunyan threw aside his pine tree beard brush and jumped to his feet with a great shout.

"'What greater work could be done in Real America than to make logs form trees?' he cried. "Logging! I shall invent this industry and make it the greatest one of all time! I shall become a figure as admired in history as any of the great ones I have read about.'"

Loggers, who were lumberjacks on the East Coast, began the press westward. First there was the long, slow cutdown in Maine and the rest of New England, with the most primitive of tools, and then, when the trees were down, the loggers crossed to the Great Lakes States, to Michigan and Wisconsin and Minnesota. The forests there were mostly white pine, which fell shockingly easy and fast, and the loggers ran south, to the southern pine

From *Stepping Westward.* Copyright © 1991, by Sallie Tisdale. Reprinted and excerpted by arrangement with Henry Holt & Company, Inc.

and cypress, and then that was gone, too. They began to talk of "the Big Clearing."

Rumors about the far Northwest, where the trees were so big — bigger, taller, tougher, thicker, and harder than anywhere else — were at first discounted as simple loggers' lies. But the itinerant lumberjacks found their way west, and found the rumors to be true. These woods, these trees, could never be cut down. "Hell, man, there was plenty of timber, timber without end, just over the Hump, and by the Holy Old Mackinaw, they'd cut her, cut her close, wide, and handsome!" So said Stewart Holbrook.

Grays Harbor, named for Robert Gray, was the best stand of all, perhaps best in the world: three to four million board feet in every forty acres, twenty million to a quarter section. The trees beat any bet a logger had made, and they were all lined up on the convenient hill-sides for their chance to slide into the deep, cool water. Lindbergh's "Spirit of St. Louis" was made from Sitka spruce cut down here, and somehow that suited everyone: Grays Harbor flew, man, it was the place to be. It was so grand, they said, "you can't lie fast enough to keep up with the honest facts." Grays Harbor was a game, a boys' wrestling match, down and sweaty in the dirt. Heaven would be Grays Harbor, a large bay on the coast of Washington: endless hills of Douglas fir so tall it made the sky look wooded, and the swearing of the bullwhackers at their oxen so obscene the bark on the younger trees curled up in shock.

It was the towns and mills of Grays Harbor that complained most particularly about the loss of timber when the Olympic National Park was created. In the late 1800s, complaints first were voiced that the amount of timber was in danger of disappearing. Decade by decade, in a kind of ritual, the timber and mill owners warned that massive unemployment was right around the corner. By 1937, the biggest trees were gone and the mills that had once tooled up to accommodate the huge logs of the Olympic Peninsula had to tool down again for the smaller ones that remained. Men who had managed to stay working through the Depression would be out of work. (Some men kept themselves working in the Depression by setting forest fires, and then getting hired to put them out.) More warnings: Grays Harbor would become nothing but ghost towns. It hasn't happened yet.

The towns of Grays Harbor, such as Hoquiam and Aberdeen, are sprawling and untidy. They are commonplace towns. There's something masculine about them, like apartments inhabited by young men who haven't got a feel for the extra touch. They are dull, mediocre, undecorative. Almost every watery view is marred by piles of logs and steaming mills. The standing trees are little oaks and maples now, and fuzzy shrubs, and seeing them, I find myself missing a forest I have never seen, knowing it was here. I never pass through without a sense of how small dreams can be.

There are different ways to talk about the impact of modern logging; one book mentions without elaborating that hundreds of thousands of acres in the Pacific Northwest "were converted to non-forest land" in the sixties. The state maps of Oregon and Washington and Idaho persist in outlining national and state forests in green, a cheering bit of art. And when I compare those state maps to the maps of other states — New York, Michigan, Maine — I am cheered twice, seeing how large are the irregular green ovals and squares out West, how few and small the forests in the East. But the green is only ink, and the reason Michigan and Maine and New York haven't got big state and national forests is because they cut them down.

Complaints of lowered cuts and increasing wilderness set-asides — which reduce the amount of timber cut by as much as one-fourth — fail to acknowledge that even after the reduction, the cuts are higher than ever before. Billions of board feet of timber still come out of the Northwest's national forests every year; the harvest from federal land in Oregon was actually higher in 1989 than in 1979. But the complaints are ever of reductions, reduced yields, set-asides, too much wilderness, too much saved. In his book celebrating the ecology of old growth, the writer David Kelly asks of the logger's term "harvest" if it is possible to say, "We can harvest what we didn't plant and don't plan to let grow back." The buffer strips are so thin you can see the clear-cuts through the branches at fifty-five miles an hour. No flier can suspend the disbelief required.

Not long after loggers got established in the region, signs showed up in store windows: NO CALKED BOOTS ALLOWED HERE. There are different signs in the stores of Forks, Washington, now. Forks, the most western incorporated town in the contiguous United States, is almost wholly dependent on logging. It rides the border of the Olympic National forest and is only a few miles from the Olympic National Park, and in the winter drinks in almost ten feet of rain. The hills around Forks are completely nude, and slash covers the draws and valleys on either side of Highway 101.

The older clear-cuts are softened with pink foxglove and little vine maples and soft green shrubs, and now and then the velvety short cones of newly planted trees. The ragged stumps are gradually turning grey and disappearing into the new grass.

The *Jobs Rated Almanac* of 1988 lists 250 careers. Reading the list makes me think of Forks up against what's left of its woods. The *Almanac* lists professions in order of desirability, dropping rapidly from Lawyer and Architect to Teacher and Nurse. You have to read almost to the bottom before you feel you're in the Northwest: Lumberjack is number 214, followed farther down by Farmer, then Dairy Farmer, Cowboy (way down at number 245), Fisherman, and, bringing up the rear, that staple of the Northwest agricultural industry, number 250, Migrant Worker. The timber industry — which is not the same as the timber worker — is happy to let the arguments over the future of our remaining forests turn into an argument over jobs. Save trees or save jobs? This way, the industry is represented by the average man, the millworker and logger with a high school education, a wife and small children, scared to death of unemployment. But the comparison — trees versus jobs — is fallacious. It is even wicked. It is undeniable that the current rate of logging in the Northwest is eliminating the forests. There is nothing sustained or sustainable about the level of logging that the Northwest has suffered in the last century, and that translates directly into unemployment. If not now, then in three, or ten, or fifteen years, many of the loggers and millworkers will be out of work because they will be out of trees. (There are people in the industry who hear that statement and point accusingly at the Olympic National Park, at the slopes of Mount Rainier, at the small bits of wilderness clustered around the region, and ask why that, too, can't be cut.) Reducing the yields, practicing less "efficient" methods, setting aside large areas to be preserved forever — these are such small things. So little to do in light of what has already been done.

Forks calls itself the timber capital of the world. It has a little tourist business, mostly fishermen coming to the nearby wild coast, or retired couples touring the Hoh Valley, coming through Forks because you can't get around the Olympic wilderness any other way. The stores now have posters that say, TIE A YELLOW RIBBON FOR THE WORKING MAN, and there are yellow ribbons on lamp poles and trees and doorknobs. All around the Northwest there have been Yellow Ribbon rallies since the issue began to heat up in 1989. That was the year it became clear that the northern spotted owl was endangered by logging, and that the species could not be saved without sweeping changes in the amount and kind of logging being done. Since then, almost no issue stirs such anger and passion here. Spotted owls have been shot, crucified, hung, and their corpses mailed to various people perceived as environmentalists. Some of the latter have chained themselves to trees, camped in the crowns of trees slated for cutting, laid down in front of trucks and been arrested by the hundreds. In the Yellow Ribbon rallies, three hundred, six hundred, sometimes twelve hundred log trucks in a line rumble through small towns and through the main thoroughfares of cities for an afternoon, their drivers and passengers hungry, angry, impotent.

In the center of the main street of Forks, which is Highway 101 and crossed every minute or two by roaring, loaded logging trucks, is a section of a Sitka spruce tree. It is a log cut from a tree thirty-seven feet in circumference and 256 feet tall. That's quite a bit taller than the standing champion Sitka spruce.

Every business, every office and restaurant in Forks has a sign in the window. Some say WE SUPPORT THE TIMBER INDUSTRY, others, WE ARE SUPPORTED BY THE TIMBER INDUSTRY. In the empty windows of one of the many empty storefronts, a line of children's posters — SAVE A LOGGER — EAT A OWL. One in neat black crayon, with a childish picture of a tree and a man: A SPOTTED OWL NEEDS HUNDREDS OF ACRES TO LIVE — WHY CAN'T I HAVE SOME OF THAT LAND TO LIVE ON? AM I IMPORTANT?

At the end of a fifteen-mile gravel road a little farther south in the Olympics, I recently found more slogans. The road entered the park and had no houses, no buildings at all, and at its end I found only a closed ranger station, the doors locked and the curtains pulled, the grass overgrown and weedy. The road gave way to several narrow, muddy trails, one crossing a wide, deceptively quiet river to the section of forest where the world's largest-known Douglas fir stands. At the trailhead was a latrine, and on the inside of the door a mass of graffiti, hostile and sharp : STUMPS SUCK. IF YOU HATE LOGGERS USE DIRT FOR YOUR TOILET PAPER. LOGGERS GET OUT.

The loggers in Forks — which celebrated James Watts Appreciation Day in 1983 — like loggers all around the Northwest, would like to blame the restrictions of wilderness advocates for their troubles, though some are aware of the problem of log exports. About eighty-four million board feet of timber comes out of this district every year, along with as much as two hundred million board feet more from state and private lands nearby. Logs cut from federal lands west of the 100th meridian cannot be exported. (There are exceptions to the ban, notably those which allow Port Orford cedar, a rare species, to be exported, and the small exception exempting Alaska from the ban completely.) Loggers still cut on private lands long after the millworkers are out of work; the logs roll down to the water and straight to Japan, which pays a higher price for the older straightest trees than any other market.

They've done so for a very long time; log exports began around the time the first tree was cut here, and people have alternately praised and blamed the countries of the Far East for our problems ever since. But exports are just part of the problem. Overcutting — cutting trees faster than they could be replaced — and overproduction — milling more timber or cutting more logs than the market could absorb — have been problems from the first time the first mill in the region closed down for want of customers. It is a regular, almost ritual complaint, this complaint of lost jobs, closed mills, towns disappearing into history because of government restrictions and environmental fanaticism. (Somewhat newer, but heard before, is blaming child abuse, wife battering, and suicide on restricted access to trees.) Meanwhile, the timber companies near Forks are predicting a shortfall by the year 2000 — a period when the old trees will all be gone and the second growth not yet big enough to cut. The amount of private timber was already falling off before the current rage over the northern spotted owl and other concerns about saving old growth began.

The loggers and millworkers are only pawns — we are all pawns here, where timber mined like gold is sold by distant conglomerates. We are marks in the game. We sell the Japanese our best, most irreplaceable trees, and they sell us electronic equipment and cars. The Northwest Passage is now realized, and the Northwest has become the Third World country instead of the other way around.

After a few days in Forks, I found myself slipping into the Missouri accent of my mother and grandmother, a product of their own grandmothers. It's soft and vowel-heavy and slow, and my mother fell into it only when she was most at ease. Those long-forgotten relatives east of the Mississippi go ghosting by when I'm in a place like Forks, which is, after all, so much like Yreka, my home town, and the places of memory. The streets are wide, the sidewalks run out after a few blocs and turn to dust, commerce is social and slow, and the minimarts sell hunting magazines and chewing tobacco along with corn chips and beer. Little towns, with big yards; in the yards are dogs, and sometimes goats, horses, and geese, and always television antennas and woodpiles covered with tarps flapping in the wind. The driveways are gravel and people drive trucks. Little gift shops, pizza parlors, grocery stores and gas stations, coffee shops and vacant lots like the vacant lots in every other little town in the country. Here there are also mills and chainsaw repair shops. Sweetness without irony — steadiness and nothing unknown. Even the wavering recession in Forks seems familiar, just another of the small recognitions that pop open for me here. If I felt like a voyeur here, then I'm a voyeur to my own history. If I'm an interloper in Forks, I'm an interloper in Yreka, in my own childhood, in my own memory.

I wandered into a little gift shop in Forks and fell into conversation with a man while we looked over salt shakers and oven mitts. He was wearing wide red suspenders with the words SPOTTED OWL HUNTER, a flannel shirt, jeans and leather boots. He was about my age, a good-looking, long-haired, lanky blond man. We chatted about Forks, and I made up little lies to explain my presence and told him of my own past, the little shivers of remembrance his town evoked. He nodded, smiled, turned over a ceramic bowl to see the price. It was the middle of the morning on a weekday, and I could only imagine his leisurely, pointless wandering to be that of the unemployed.

He is suspicious, I think; he is skeptical of my motives in being in Forks, in talking with him. I wanted to tell him that I'd known him all my life, that we were peers. I dated him, he's my brother, my neighbor all grown up. I smoked pot with him in high school and rode in the back of his old Buick to go swimming in the creek. He is as familiar to me as the streets of Forks. And our friendly, flirtatious talk is ringed with tension.

Rarely have I felt such a sense of being stuck on one side of an idea, whether I wanted to be or not. I am what he might call a "tree hugger," one of the less derisive terms coined lately by cornered people determined to go down with pride. We lack a common aesthetic, this man and I. I am inclined toward the raw and disused; I have faith in chaos. I imagine — without asking, reading the message on his red suspenders — that he has a separate faith, a trust in mechanism, an inclination toward control. He sees the miles of clear-cuts north of town, and sees work done, a project finished — and a field of slash to burn and Douglas-fir seedlings to plant. I see a scene of devastation and loss; I see Soleduck cut down, the Hoh Valley turned bare. I see something that cannot be made lovely by any cast of light or change of season. I see a kind of physical and psychological violence. It is I who am tense here, who am sad, and I who end the conversation and find my way back to the Forks Motel.

Author's note: The Paul Bunyan quotation in this article is taken from *Paul Bunyan* by James Stevens, Knopf, 1925.

CLEARCUT

PHOTOGRAPHS by CHRISTOPHER HARRIS

Jackman, Maine — *above*
Forest Road 70, Washington — *page 30*
Stimson, Washington — *page 31*
Darrington, Washington — *page 32*

31

THE ISLANd WiThiN

by RicHARd NElSON

After a long hike, taking the easy routes of deer trails, we move into a stand of shore pine that ends beside a half-overgrown logging road. This is the first sign of human activity since we left camp, and it indicates we're approaching the clearcut valley. The road follows a narrow band of muskeg that has all the delicate loveliness of a Japanese garden, with reflecting ponds and twisted pines in bonsai shapes. Farther on, it cuts through an alder thicket and runs up a steep, forested slope. A dense flock of birds sprays into the high trees, twittering like canaries, hundreds of them, agitated and nervous, moving so quickly they're difficult to hold for long in the binoculars.

The birds are everywhere, hanging upside down from the twigs and working furiously on spruce cones. Each one plucks and twists at its cone, shaking loose the thin scales and letting them fall. The air is filled with a flutter of brown scales. I recognize the sparrow-sized pine siskins immediately, then identify the larger birds as white-winged crossbills. I've never had a good look at a crossbill before, but the hillside roadway gives an easy view into the tree crowns, where bright red males and olive females swarm through the boughs. With some patience, I can discern the tips of their beaks, which crisscross instead of fitting together like an ordinary bird's. This allows the crossbill to pry the scales apart and insert its tongue to extract seeds embedded deep within. Once again, I'm reminded that tropical animals aren't the only ones who have added a little adventure to their evolution. Suddenly the whole flock spills out from the trees and disappears, like bees following their queen.

After another half-mile, a slot appears in the road ahead. As we approach,

From *The Island Within.* © 1989. Published in the United States by Vintage Books, a division of Random House, Inc., New York, 1991. Originally published in hardcover by North Point Press, California, in 1989. Reprinted by permission of Susan Bergholz Literary Services, New York.

it widens to a gateway out of the forest — a sudden, shorn edge where the trees and moss end, and where the dark, dour sky slumps down against a barren hillside strewn with slash and decay. Oversized snowflakes blotch against my face and neck, and the breeze chills through me. I look ahead, then look back toward the trees, breathless and anxious, almost wishing I hadn't come. It's the same foreboding I sometimes feel in the depths of sleep, when a blissful dream slowly degenerates into a nightmare; I am carried helplessly along, dimly hoping it's only a dream, but unable to awaken myself and escape.

The road angles into a wasteland of hoary trunks and twisted wooden shards, pitched together in convulsed disarray, with knots of shoulder-high brush pressing in along both sides. Fans of mud and ash splay across the roadway beneath rilled cutbanks. In one place, the lower side has slumped away and left ten feet of culvert hanging in midair, spewing brown water over the naked bank and into a runnel thirty feet below.

A tall snag clawed with dead branches stands atop the hill. I decide to hike up toward it rather than walk farther along the road. At first, it's a relief to be in the brush, where I can touch something alive, and where my attention is focused on the next footstep rather than the surrounding view. But thirty yards into it, I realize that moving through a clearcut is unlike anything I've ever tried before. The ground is covered with a nearly impenetrable confusion of branches, roots, sticks, limbs, stumps, blocks, poles, and trunks, in every possible size, all gray and fibrous and rotting, all thrown together in a chaotic mass and interwoven with a tangle of brittle bushes.

An astonishing amount of wood was left here to decay, including whole trees, hundreds of them in this one clearcut alone. Some flaw must have made them unusable even for pulp, but they were felled nonetheless, apparently so the others would be easier to drag out. Not a single living tree above sapling size stands in the thirty or forty acres around me.

I creep over the slippery trunks and crawl beneath them, slip and stumble across gridworks of slash, and worm through close-growing salmonberry, menziesia, and huckleberry. Even Shungnak struggles with her footing, but she gets around far better than I do, moving like a weasel through a maze of small holes and tunnels. I can tell where she is by the noise she makes in the brush, but only see her when she comes to my whistle. In some places I walk along huge, bridging trunks, but they're slick and perilous, and I risk falling onto a deadly skewer of wood below. I save myself from one misstep by grabbing the nearest branch, which turns out to be devil's club, festooned with spines that would do credit to any cactus. We also cross dozens of little washes that run over beds of coarse ash and gravel. There are no mossy banks, no spongy seeps, just water on bare earth. By the time we near the top I am strained, sweating, sore, frustrated, and exhausted. It has taken me almost an hour to cross a few hundred yards of this crippled land.

I've heard no sound except my own unhappy voice since we entered the clearcut, but now a winter wren's song pours up from a nearby patch of young alders. I usually love to hear wrens, especially during the silence of winter. But in this topsy-turvy place the reedy, contorted phrases, rattling against the beaten hill, seem like angry words in some bewildering foreign tongue. I picture a small, brown-skimmed man, shaking his fist at the sky from the edge of a bombed and cratered field.

A large stump raised six feet above the ground on buttressed roots offers a good lookout. The man who felled this tree cut two deep notches in its base, which I use to clamber on top. It's about five feet in diameter and nearly flat, except for a straight ridge across the center where the cutter left hinge wood to direct the tree's fall. The surface is soggy and checked, but still ridged with concentric growth rings. On hands and knees, nose almost touching the wood, using my knife blade as a pointer, I start to count. In a short while, I know the tree died in its four hundred and twenty-third year.

I stand to see the whole forest of stumps. It looks like an enormous grave-yard, covered with weathered markers made from the remains of its own dead. Along the slope nearby is a straight line of four stumps lifted on con-voluted roots, like severed hands still clasping a nearly vanished mother log. Many of the surrounding stumps are smaller than my platform, but others are as large or larger. A gathering of ancients once stood here. Now it re-minds me of a prairie in the last century, strewn with the bleached bones of buffalo. Crowded around the clearcut's edges are tall trees that seem to press forward like curious, bewildered gawkers.

Two centuries ago, it would have taken the Native people who lived here several days to fell a tree like this one, and weeks or months to wedge it into planks. Earlier in this century, the handloggers could pull their huge cross-cut saws through it in a couple of hours. But like the Native Americans be-fore, they selected only the best trees and left the others. Now I gaze into a valley miles deep, laid bare to its high slopes, with only patches of living tim-ber left between the clearcut swaths.

Where I stand now, a great tree once grew. The circles that mark the cen-turies of its life surround me, and I dream back through them. It's difficult to imagine the beginnings — perhaps a seed that fell from a flurry of cross-bills like those I saw a while ago. More difficult still is the incomprehensible distance of time this tree crossed, as it grew from a limber switch on the forest floor to a tree perhaps 150 feet tall and weighing dozens of tons. Another way to measure the scope of its life is in terms of storms. Each year scores of them swept down this valley — thousands of boiling gales and blizzards in the tree's lifetime — and it withstood them all.

The man who walked up beside it some twenty years ago would have seemed no more significant than a puff of air on a summer afternoon.

Perhaps thin shafts of light shone down onto the forest floor that day, and danced on the velvet moss. I wonder what that man might have thought, as he looked into the tree's heights and prepared to bring it down. Perhaps he thought only about the job at hand, or his aching back, or how long it was until lunch. I would like to believe he gave some consideration to the tree itself, to its death and his responsibilities toward it, as he pulled the cord that set his chain saw blaring.

The great, severed tree cut an arc across the sky and thundered down through its neighbors, sending a quake deep into the earth and a roar up against the valley walls. And while the tree was limbed and bucked, dozens of other men worked along the clearcut's advancing front, as a steady stream of trucks hauled the logs away.

A Koyukon man named Joe Stevens once took me with him to cut birch for a dog sled and snowshoes. Each time we found a tall, straight tree with clear bark, he made a vertical slice in the trunk and pulled out a thin strip of wood to check the straightness of its grain. When we finally came across a tree he wanted to cut, Joe said, "I don't care how smart a guy is, or how much he knows about birch. If he acts the wrong way — he treats his birch like it's nothing — after that he can walk right by a good tree and wouldn't see it." Later on, he showed me several giant, old birches with narrow scars on their trunks, where someone had checked the grain many years ago. In the same stand, he pointed out a stump that had been felled with an ax, and explained that Chief Abraham used to get birch here before the river made a new channel and left his fish camp on a dry slough.

Joe and I bucked the tree into logs and loaded them on a sled, then hauled them to the village and took them inside his house. It was important to peel the bark in a warm place, he said, because the tree still had life and awareness in it. Stripping the log outside would expose its nakedness to the winter cold and offend its spirit. The next day, he took the logs out and buried them under the snow, where they would be sheltered until he could split them into lumber. Later on, when Joe carved pieces of the birch to make snowshoe frames, I tried to help by putting the shavings in a fire. His urgent voice stopped me: "Oldtimers say we shouldn't burn snowshoe shavings. We put those back in the woods, away from any trails, where nobody will bother them. If we do that, we'll be able to find good birch again next time."

The clearcut valley rumbled like an industrial city through a full decade of summers, as the island's living flesh was stripped away. Tugs pulled great rafts of logs from Deadfall Bay, through tide-slick channels toward the mill, where they were ground into pulp and slurried aboard ships bound for Japan. Within a few months, the tree that took four centuries to grow was transformed into newspapers, read by commuters on afternoon trains, and then tossed away.

I think of the men who worked here, walking down this hill at the day's end, heading home to their families in the camp beside Deadfall Bay. I could judge them harshly indeed, and think myself closer to the image of Joe Stevens; but that would be a mistake. The loggers were people just like me, not henchmen soldiers in a rebel army, their pockets filled with human souvenirs. They probably loved working in the woods and found their greatest pleasures in the outdoors. I once had a neighbor who was a logger all his life, worked in these very clearcuts, and lost most of his hearing to the chain saw's roar. He was as fine a man as I could hope to meet. And he lived by the conscience of Western culture — that the forest is here for taking, in whatever way humanity sees fit.

The decaying stump is now a witness stand, where I pass judgment on myself. I hold few convictions so deeply as my belief that a profound transgression was committed here, by devastating an entire forest rather than taking from it selectively and in moderation. Yet whatever judgment I might make against those who cut it down I must also make against myself. I belong to the same nation, speak the same language, vote in the same elections, share many of the same values, avail myself of the same technology, and owe much of my existence to the same vast system of global exchange. There is no refuge in blaming only the loggers or their industry or the government that consigned this forest to them. The entire society — one in which I take active membership — holds responsibility for laying this valley bare.

The most I can do is strive toward a separate kind of conscience, listen to an older and more tested wisdom, participate minimally in a system that debases its own sustaining environment, work toward a different future, and hope that someday all will be pardoned.

A familiar voice speaks agreement. I squint up into the sleet as a black specter turns and soars above, head cocked to examine me. A crack of light shows through his opened beak; his throat fluffs out with each croak; downy feathers on his back lift in the wind; an ominous hiss arises from his indigo wings. Grandfather Raven surveys what remains of his creation, and I am the last human alive. But he drifts away and disappears beyond the mountainside, still only keeping watch, patient, waiting.

I try to take encouragement form the ten-foot hemlock and spruce saplings scattered across the hillside. Interestingly, no tender young have taken root atop the flat stumps and mossless trunks. Some of the fast-growing alders are twenty feet tall, but in winter they add to the feeling of barrenness and death. Their thin, crooked branches scratch against the darkened clouds and rattle in the wind. The whole landscape is like a cooling corpse, with new life struggling up between its fingers. If I live a long time, I might see this hillside covered with the beginnings of a new forest. Left alone for a few centuries, the trees would form a high canopy with scattered openings. Protected from the deep snows of open country, deer would again survive the pinch of winter by retreating into the forest. The whole community of dispossessed animals would return: red squirrel, marten, great horned owl, hairy woodpecker, golden-crowned kinglet, pine siskin, blue grouse, and the seed-shedding crossbills. In streams cleared of sediment by moss-filtered runoff, swarms of salmon would spawn once more, hunted by brown bears who emerged from the cool woods.

There is comfort in knowing another giant tree could replace the one that stood here, even though it would take centuries of unfettered growth. I wish I could sink down into the earth and wait, listen for the bird voices to awaken me, rise from beneath the moss, and find myself sheltered by resplendent boughs. And in this world beyond imagination, such inordinate excesses toward nature will have become unthinkable.

A LETTER HOME

by William Woodall

Dear Mark,

Late June. 10:00 a.m. Already my Korean apartment is hot and humid. The light gray flowers in the wallpaper are wilting against the darker gray background as they struggle vertically up the walls and droop diagonally across the ceiling. I think about my summer vacation in Idaho, empty space, and people I'll visit, and wish for the next nine days to pass now.

I've visited a few tourist sites during my first semester here as a way of relaxing. But it's always with students or other members of the faculty. With or without them, though, I'm rarely alone: this is the third most densely populated country in the world. Forty million people in a space half the size of Idaho. The national parks contain beautiful temples, tens of thousands of forty-year-old trees the same size, and hundreds of thousands of people. Pick a steep, rocky trail in any one of them on any Saturday or Sunday and you'll be moved along by a continuous queue of hikers, one line — or three — going up and as many coming down. (I should note that one Sunday I was fully alone on a trail for nearly 28 seconds.)

Sometimes it's better closer to my apartment, though. I often hike out through the eastern edge of Taejon to Chicken Foot Mountain, to fill my water bottles from a spring which flows clean and sweet from its base. Taejon is a city of one million people that cries, pounds, honks, and groans constantly under the weight of overcrowding, industrialization, and construction. We all boil our tap water, buy bottled water, or go to this or other springs to have something decent to drink.

This last option suits me the best. The exercise helps me manage stress, and the hiking trails on this small mountain aren't "developed" yet. They will be, though, before I finish my sojourn here at the end of 1992. Already they've begun construction on a cable car to haul Koreans and tourists alike to the top. The chanting of Buddhist monks in a small, old temple is now accompanied daily by the drone and grind of the diesel generator and small winch that move materials up the steep slope.

Most days I walk past this temple and on up the mountain. If I take the right fork off the main trail I avoid the rest of the construction and most of the people. I loop around through an open area of scrub pine and up to a small saddle about three-fourths of the way to the top. Five hundred yards past there I drop down slightly as I come to a small forest of young tamaracks. The biggest one, which grows right beside a small, well-tended bunker, is about eighteen inches in diameter at its base: a good-sized tree for this country. When the wind is just right I can sit here and not hear the city on the other side of the ridge. It feels almost like an Idaho forest, except for the occasional sound of M-16's.

On the way back to town I fill my bottles. Then it's twenty minutes by bus or twice that on foot back to my apartment. I just made this trip yesterday, so it's very clear in my mind. What's also very clear is that there is no wilderness here. I have a chance to be alone in the forest only if I take this walk on a weekday. The only undeveloped land in this country lies in the Demilitarized Zone, the buffer with North Korea. Unfortunately, the tour-bus schedule is pretty irregular.

Like Thoreau, then, "I wish to speak a word for Nature, for absolute freedom and wildness." Because I've been doing too much of my "walking" in the city, I believe more strongly now "in the forest and meadow," that life, indeed, "consists with wildness."

That's what I think as I sit sweating in my rundown apartment. In the middle of a noisy, Asian city. In a country where wilderness is more than an endangered species. Where the manifold grayness of the city and the lack of darkness and silence some days threaten to engulf me.

I dream about the wilderness in Idaho, lingering mentally in places I've never been and to which I may never go. The idea of such visits and the images wash over me like the gentle reassurance of a lover's slow, confident caress. Because right now, it helps me just to know it's there.

Bill

TOM FRANKS

THE GREATEST EXTINCTION

by Peter Douglas Ward

As you walk the land, bone-dry land, it takes a long reach of the imagination to believe that a shallow sea once existed here. And yet such was the case in this West Texas desert. You are surrounded by sagebrush and tumbleweed, and although it is still early spring, the sun already cooks the dusty terrain. You are hiking up through a dry wash, crossing a wide alluvial fan deposited by Bone Springs. Low rocky outcroppings can be seen crumbling, but the fine shales are too weathered to yield much insight into the ancient sea of their origin. As the morning wears on you climb higher still, passing upward into the multicolored rocks of Cherry canyon and finally up into Brushy Canyon. At these higher elevations you find more consolidated rock, and sea fossils galore: mostly brachiopods everywhere, but species very different from those of the Ordovician-aged Ohio Valley. You are high above the desert floor now, and the West Texas winds blow ceaselessly. Buzzards wheel in giant circles over your head, hoping you will join the long-dead brachiopods in the next world perhaps. But your attention is entirely on the giant cliff of searing white rocks thrusting upward above the soft shales you stand on, white limestones of Late Permian age. You finally reach the base of these white cliffs and begin the demolition for which you have come. With hammer and chisel you break off large hunks of white limestone and peer with wonder at an abundance of fossils, packed into every nook of the rock, a carnival of long-extinct creatures. You see beadlike fossils of a type completely foreign to you, the remains of calcareous sponges once common. Bits of calcareous algae and bryozoans are also evident, along

43

From *On Methuselah's Trail* by Peter Douglas Ward. Copyright © 1992 by Peter Douglas Ward. Reprinted by permission of W.H. Freeman and Company.

with fragments of long-extinct corals. And interdispersed with this richness you find uncountable brachiopod shells. You are collecting El Capitan, a giant block of limestone extending from West Texas to New Mexico, the remains of a giant barrier reef complex that made up the southern coastline of North America about 250 million years ago. You are seeing the remains of what was perhaps the largest single reef system ever to exist, a structure that would have dwarfed even the present-day Great Barrier Reef system of Australia. It is a sad monument in a way, for this great, ancient burial ground records the last flowering of Paleozoic life before the Fall — the single greatest mass extinction recorded in rock history, which occurred at the end of the Permian Period. Within several millions of years after the rocks around you were deposited, most of these species became extinct, along with as many as 95 percent of all other species on earth. The Fall ended the Paleozoic Era, and with it the hegemony of the brachiopods.

It is somewhat ironic that this greatest of known extinctions has received so little attention in relation to other such events in the earth's past, particularly the extinction at the end of the Cretaceous Period, 65 million years ago, which did in the dinosaurs and much else. Perhaps this neglect can be attributed to the much greater age of the Permian event, for it occurred almost 250 million years ago. Or perhaps it came about because the creatures it affected are so little known in comparison with the dinosaurs. But let no one be fooled — the extinctions that closed out the Mesozoic Era were but a shadow of the grim reaping that occurred at the end of the Paleozoic. At the end of the Permian the face of death was to be seen everywhere, both on land and in the sea. Only one of every ten species survived the end of the Permian.

What caused this mass dying? There is no evidence of great volcanic paroxysms, or of giant meteors flaming through the atmosphere to strike the earth with deadly force. Earth scientists familiar with this extinction don't even believe that it occurred rapidly; most of them suspect that the event lasted longer than a million years, and may have gone on for more than 10 million years. This great death seems to have been triggered by no extraterrestrial event, such as the crashing to earth of a meteor or comet, but by events caused by the changing face of the earth itself. The agents of death at the end of the Permian Period appear to have been a change in climate and a lowering of the sea level, both created in large part by the positions of the continents.

Geologists would very much like to know what coordinates or controls the movement of the continents. The great revolutionary theory of plate tectonics, formulated in the early 1960s, has shown that the sea floor spreads and huge regions of the earth's surface drift a few inches each year. These huge plates, some carrying continents, some not, move about over the surface of the globe like children in bumper cars.

At the end of the Paleozoic Era all of the continental masses we know today coalesced into one huge supercontinent. For the only time that we know of (no such thing has happened before or since), all of the major continental blocks lay welded together.

It took tens of millions of years for the various continents to converge in this supercontinent, which has been named Pangea. As the various land masses came together, the climate of the world changed drastically. The interiors of continents in our world are mainly places of climate extremes — hot summers and cold, harsh winters. As the continents merged, the interior areas cut off from the moderating influence of the seas became ever larger. These continental interiors must have been among the least hospitable places in all the long history of our earth. The strata found from these environments tell a tale of drifting sand and salt deposits, stark testimony of aridity. And as the world climate changed during this process, giant ice sheets began to grow over both the north and south polar regions. One of the greatest glaciations in the history of the earth unfolded. As the great ice sheets advanced, sucking up moisture from the air and sea, the level of the seas began to drop, rapidly draining the most favored of marine habitats, the shallow shelf seas of the world, where nutrients and light are so abundant. No wonder so many species on land and sea began to die. By late-Permian time only the tropics maintained a preserve of abundant animal and plant life. The giant Permian reef complex of West Texas is a last bastion of life in this long-ago late-Paleozoic world. And then that life, too, slowly died.

The list of victims of the late-Permian extinctions is long. Prominent among them were the trilobites and all of the Paleozoic corals, most crinoids, and large number of land reptiles. Among the hardest hit of all were the brachiopods. *Lingula* survived, as did a handful of articulate brachiopods. But many thousands of species of brachiopods did not.

With the start of the Mesozoic Era the few survivors faced an emptied world. The continents began to spread apart and the glaciers retreated; the sea rose and flooded the continents. The huge inland seas rich in nutrients opened up new opportunities for the rapid evolution of sea life. New species of brachiopods began to form. But history did not repeat itself: the ocean habitats did not fill with a diversity of brachiopods, as in the Paleozoic, for the newly evolving brachiopods found their old haunts already occupied: "no vacancy" signs were already hung out over the offshore, normal marine salinity environments so beloved of the Paleozoic brachiopods. The new tenants, bivalve mollusks, were so well ensconced that the brachiopods were unable to regain a toehold in their marine realm. The new masters controlled the feast of plankton; the old were sent to the ecological sidelines to eke out marginal existences in caves and deep water or, like *Lingula,* at the edge of the sea. The heyday of brachiopods was over, never to return.

Evolution is a numbers game. More bivalves than brachiopods survived the Permian extinction, so the bivalves had a headstart in repopulating the early-Mesozoic world. To make themselves unappetizing to predators, the surviving brachiopods became poisonous to eat. To find a home of their own they retreated to inhospitable habitats and strong-current areas of cold-water oceans; except for a furtive existence deep in the caves of reefs, they quit the tropics entirely. To see brachiopods today you have to be ready to dive deep into cold water.

A Day in the Life

Some days are made for diving in Puget Sound. On cold winter days you have to be crazy to put on a thick wet suit and descend into the frigid water of the fjordlike waterway of northern Washington State; in fact, with an average water temperature of about 45 degrees F, many people think you would have to be crazy to dive in there at *any* time. But on some days the air is so clear and the sun reflecting off the mirrorlike surface of the green water so warm that a dive into the rich waters of the sound seems like a perfectly sane idea.

I am mulling over such earthshaking thoughts as I pull on my long johns. I am sitting in a friend's boat, an old cabin cruiser, on a perfect July day in 1980. We are adrift off Vashon Island, a small isle about thirty miles south of Seattle. My diving buddy is an old friend, a man I have dived with for a decade. The diving fraternity in the Seattle area has been a small group for many years, although that situation, like so many others, is changing these days. We taught scuba diving classes together when I was an under-graduate in college, so there is no need on this or any other day to go through the macho exercises so beloved of many divers of our acquaintance. Which means that we are both bitching like mad about the fact that the wet suits are wet and must have shrunk (it couldn't be that our waistlines have expanded, after all), that the tanks didn't get an honest fill, that the regulators aren't breathing properly, and so on. This is ritual; we wouldn't feel good about going diving if we didn't go through this exercise. We are nearly ready now; both of us have put on our bubble suits and have swung the massive tanks on our backs. Just before rolling over the side of the boat, my friend turns to me and asks, "Hey, Doc, just what the hell *is* a brachiopod, anyway?" I give him my best raised eyebrow and fall back over the side of the boat into one of the few places on earth where these survivors from the Paleozoic Era still flourish.

I began diving when I was sixteen. I bought a fire-extinguisher bottle and a new valve for it, and a friend gave me an old double-hose regulator. I got an air fill, a mask, and a pair of fins. Thus equipped, I dived into Lake Washington alone. I will never forget the exhilaration that comes when you realize that you do *not* have to go back up after a few seconds, the sense of freedom when you take your first breath off an aqualung underwater. But it is very easy to die in the water, diving alone, not knowing or caring about embolisms or pulmonary emphysema or a score of other horrible fates. I can still scare myself silly just thinking about it. God sometimes looks after his more stupid children, and I survived to find new equipment eventually and to read some books. The equipment is a lot different now; the air suits keep you much warmer and the regulators are much more efficient. But I experienced my greatest joys with the cadged, jury-rigged outfit of my teen years as I learned the waters of Puget Sound, developing advanced skin wrinkling before my time.

No matter how good the fit of your suit, with its hood and gloves and booties, there is always some spot where at least a little cold salt water finds its way to your skin when you first hit the water. On this day I find, to my shock, that the small hole in my wet suit, very inconveniently located right above the small of my back, has not been repaired. I reorient myself after the somersaulting entry from the boat, find "up," and look for my friend. I see him in the distance. We are fortunate on this day, for the water visibility is about twenty feet — a very clear day for Puget Sound. Some days you're lucky to see your hand in front of your face. I swim over to him with good hard strokes of my fins, and hard strokes are needed, for the tidal current is still running, though rapidly diminishing, and it takes most of my strength to push upstream.

We have chosen this day because it promises little tidal change. Puget Sound is mesotidal, which means that the tides can rise or fall as much as fifteen feet in six hours. Such a rapid change in the height of the sea in a restricted body of water produces swift and powerful currents. These tidal currents are one of the main reasons that Puget Sound teems with one of the most diverse assemblages of marine creatures known on earth.

A diver can swim, at best, about one-half knot. We are both slightly heavy, and float downward together along the anchor chain, finally reaching the sandy bottom in about 20 feet of water. The bottom here is slightly rippled and pocked with rocks. The larger rocks, some as big as a football but most the size of a fist, are all covered with barnacles and mussels, and here and there the starfish that feed on them. Bright-red rock crabs scuttle among the rocks and raise menacing claws at our passage. All of the sediment here is the refuse of glaciers, the remains of the scour and gouge of the monstrously thick piles of ice so recently part of the Northwest landscape. Most of Puget Sound is bordered by high cliffs composed of sand and gravel; heavy rainfall ensures that large quantities of this material make their way into Puget Sound.

We have chosen this spot to dive because it is one of the few areas in the southern part of Puget Sound where vertical cliffs are exposed underwater; in most areas the bottom slopes downward gradually. We swim along the bottom, edging downward in colder water. Warm summer is only about 20 feet above our heads, but the salt water rapidly darkens as we move into deeper water. I can feel the increasing pressure reducing the volume of my air suit until the fabric is tightly clutching my skin, the giant invisible hand of Boyles Law reminding me of my journey into an evermore foreign land. I fumble for the valve to admit more air into my suit, and the rush of warm air is a relief. I glance at my partner, moving gracefully and silently at my side, and I am heartened by his presence. I am but a guest in this dark world, if a frequent one; no matter how often one dives into this body of water, there is always the slight sense of dread with the descent into the dark and the cold.

As we move downward over the slope we see the sediment change, and the animals too. The cobbled, rippled sand gives way to a finer, purer sand, and then to silt. At 30 feet we enter a magical realm, a forest of bright-yellow sea pens. These creatures, related to soft corals, look like plants, but they are highly integrated colonies of animals. They are about two feet high and in some places are no more than a foot apart. They endlessly filter the surrounding seawater of its cargo of plankton in this frigid place, and are themselves the food of starfish, which slowly move among them. The sea pens may be living fossils, for fossils that look much like the creatures of Puget Sound are known from the Precambrian-aged Ediacaran sandstones of Australia. Once in a while we scare a flounder off the bottom, and as we pass a sunken log a large octopus disappears into the rotted wood, the site of its den betrayed by a pile of crustacean refuse. Finally, at a depth of about 50 feet, we come to the edge of a great underwater cliff.

I float over the edge, weightless, and ready the camera I have brought along. My underwater Nikonos has been a reliable friend for many years and has witnessed memorable scenes. I screw in the appropriate settings in the dim light and ready the attached strobe, for the available light down here is far too dim for picture taking. My friend has a large underwater light, now on, and moves over the side with me. We let a little air out of our suits to reduce our buoyancy and float down toward the absolute blackness beneath us. At about 75 feet I move in close against the wall and see the creatures I have come to collect.

The sheer wall here is another legacy of the glaciers, and of the tidal currents as well. It is composed of cobbles and boulders of Pleistocene glacier outwash, sediments shaped and eroded first by the glaciers and then by the tidal currents that wash back and forth four times a day. I look closely at this underwater wall and see countless brachiopods, each shell gaping slightly, drawing in seawater from each side and pouring it out of the front. The brachs are at most about an inch long, and in the glare of my friend's light I see dull brown shells with bright-orange interiors. Each individual brachiopod is strongly anchored to the wall with a thin proteinaceous tether, called a pedicle — its lifeline. If ever this cord is broken, the brachiopod cannot reattach itself, and will die. The cord is tough, and the cement attaching it to the rock surface is tougher yet. Many scientists and chemists have pondered the chemistry of this glue, so strong that it makes our synthetic cements seem ludicrous by comparison. I set up a photo at close range; the ensuing strobe blasts the surrounding area into whiteness for the briefest of moments. I wonder if these eyeless shellfish can detect this sudden release of energy on any level at all, and the thought leaves me cold. Our lives are controlled largely by light, and we define our world mostly in terms of its visual context; it seems (from my anthropocentric viewpoint) so alien to confront a creature that has never made the slightest evolutionary accommodation to light. As my eyes readjust to the darkness I look again at the pale shells on the wall before me. They grow slowly, these brachiopods, taking five to seven years to reach their full length of about an inch. Almost everything we know about their natural history has come from the work of one man, Charles Thayer of the University of Pennsylvania, and I wish Charlie were here now to explain just what it is I am seeing on this deep wall. Is this an ancient brachiopod population? A new one? What is its past? And what of its future? I have long promised this dive to Charlie, to show him this wall.

We have drifted ever deeper for I want to map the face of the wall and learn the depths at which the brachiopods drop out. But they stay present in undiminishing numbers as we drop below 100 feet. It's very dark now and very cold; the great pressure requires us to admit much more air into our dry suits to maintain neutral buoyancy. Air is now a consideration, for each breath we take pulls a large column of compressed air from our tanks; at this depth we're going through air at a rapid clip. We also must worry a bit about the nitrogen uptake of our bodies; we have only twenty minutes at most. Any longer and we'll have to decompress on our way up if we're to avoid the bends.

I can keep track of my friend because of his light. Even so, we must take great care to stay together, for the visibility is all but nil. Signals of many kinds tell me it's time to go home: my watch tells me how long I've been down here; the pressure gauge on my tank tells me of the relentless dwindling of the life-giving air on my back; my body temperature, despite the cumbersome dry suit, is rapidly dropping, and I'm beginning to shake. Our depth has also brought a slight edge of nitrogen narcosis, leading to a foreboding that cannot be erased. But mostly I'm concerned about the tidal current. For as long as we have been down here, more than fifteen minutes now, the water has been virtually still: we planned this dive for the time of slack water, the cusp between the tides, when the great volumes of seawater are held in the balance. But now I begin to feel the tug of the outgoing tide start to push against me. We must leave now if we are to get back to our boat. I move back to the wall and with my knife dislodge several brachiopods to take back to the aquarium at my university. I place them in my goody bag and turn to look at my friend. With shock I realize that he dropped down beneath me; I can't see him, but the stream of bubbles coming up around me indicates his position. I hear the twang of his spear gun firing. The noise, as usual, gives no hint of direction. I drop down through the stream of his rising bubbles and find him struggling with an enormous ling cod, the top carnivore of this world. The fish is speared but not dead, and it struggles mightily. There is little I can do but watch as my friend finally subdues the fish and attaches it to a stringer dangling from his weight belt. I give him a vigorous thumbs-up sign. He returns a hearty nod and we begin our ascent into the light. But the current is pushing with a vengeance now, and as we rise we are pulled northward. It's useless to try to swim back against the current; that mistake is often fatal to divers in this area. Instead we move up the wall until we reach the lip and then strike towards shore, now being carried swiftly by the relentless current. It is this current that brought the brachiopods to this place, this swift river of seawater rich in suspended organic material and pastures of plankton, a movable feast perfect for a tiny creature firmly anchored to the substrate.

With relief we finally reach the 20-foot depth once again, with its warmth and light. We ascend the last feet and break surface to see our boat several hundred yards to the south. We swim to the beach, kicking hard now, perpendicular to the direction of the current. We are tired as we flop on the shore, but before trudging down the beach and then swimming out to the boat we inspect our respective catches. I make appropriate comments about the puniness of the ling cod. My friend takes this ribbing gravely and makes a point of inspecting a brachiopod from my goody bag and dismisses it as "just a dumb clam." Then I launch into my sermon about the differences between clams and brachiopods until a wicked smile lets me know I've been caught pontificating again. "Do you mind?" my friend asks, and without waiting for a response, he wedges the end of his knife between the two shells, now firmly closed. I wince at the destruction of this prize, but he finally pops the shells open, ripping several shell-closing muscles in the process. My friend looks at the opened brachiopod with surprise. "There's nothing in here," he says, but I point out the lacy, frill-like lophophore, the specialized feeding structure that makes up the greater part of the internal organs of a brachiopod. My friend has eaten many a clam in his life, and even if he is completely ignorant of clam anatomy, he quickly realizes how different the internal anatomies of a clam and a brachiopod really are. Most people are fooled because of the similar shape and size of the shells, but once past the shell, you are obviously dealing with a very different animal.

My friend holds up the remains of the now thoroughly destroyed brachiopod and has derisive things to say about how little flesh there is for so large a shell. "No wonder they're almost extinct," he mumbles, and then asks me if they are any good to eat. "Don't do it!" I tell him. My friends assures me that *anything* taken from Puget Sound waters is edible. "*Don't do it!*" I shout. He gives me his best stage sneer, the one reserved for scientists and intones his favorite condemnation of scientists and their practical ignorance: "Too much college and not enough high school." The brachiopod, remnant of one of the great stocks of life, survivor since the earliest Paleozoic, disappears into his mouth and plays its part in the ongoing process of evolution. Its death surely serves some purpose, for it greatly diminishes the probability that at least one human being will ever again try to eat a brachiopod: even before the wretched creature is halfway down, my friend turns green, and retches violently on the beach. I can't help myself; I roar with laughter. "One thing about college," I tell him when he regains his composure and control of his stomach. "At least they teach you not to eat brachiopods."

Bonebed:

Out of the scattered bone
reconstruct a herd. Scapula, femur, horncore.
Pattern. Fragment.

There is nothing complete, except the heat, even with its age
accumulated across the dark miles and absorbed in the softness of this
landscape. All those millions of years just leave us exhausted
and without conviction. Yet we return

to walk among them, the strata warm as a lived-in body, recurrent
heat in its mineral glitter, given back just as the bones
fall apart at its surface, their shapes a recollection of something organic,
something with the heat of evidence in it.

Look how the ribs lie parallel and imagine a river's parallel flow
pulling them that way. Compare the sizes of a bone known to occur
only once in each animal. What is it you know, the indirect past
shuttles through the layered Earth and if you return

at midnight, with the pallid rock still warm and the great
herd of shadows pausing on its way across what has been interpreted
as a coastal plain you will find the fleshed-out names easy to say.
Occipital condyle, where the skull rests upon the frame.

Reflected light is the real, the insistent light.

by Monty Reid

53

Dinosaur Provincial Park

A FUTURE AS BIG AS INDONESIA

by David Quammen

O nce we were a young inconsiderable species that occupied enclaves of settlement within the great world of unhumbled nature. Not so long ago, really, 15 or 20 thousand years. But we had a hypertrophied brain and an opposable thumb and a tongue that could shape many sounds. Our history had been short but extraordinary. Suddenly at some point in the recent past we'd stood upright and begun making inventions. We had invented the basket, the club, the pestle, the robe, the spear, the bowl, the hoe, the atlatl, and the cage. Soon after the cage we invented the prison and the zoo, though no one can say which came first. For millennia, then, zoos were small enclaves of captive animals held in pampered sequestration for the amusement of rich and powerful humans who lived in pampered sequestration themselves, inside those larger enclaves of settlement that existed within the still-pretty-big world of still-mainly-unhumbled nature. Eventually we invented the machete, the flint fire-starter, the plow. We invented the yoke, the saddle, the gun, the door, the concept of indoors versus outdoors, the rotisserie, the fence, the wheel, the iron pot, religion, the irrigation ditch, the chain saw, the Bic lighter, the airplane, the church key, the hood ornament, the surname, the dimension of dread as distinct from fear, and the sandwich, not necessarily in that order. Zoos became larger. They also became democratic and educational. But democracy, sad to say, is often unfriendly to nature. Meanwhile our enclaves of settlement became larger too, much larger, until those were no longer enclaves. Nature became small, fragmentary, beleaguered. And now, at the height of our puissance, it's we who've got nature surrounded.

The object-to-ground relations have reversed. Wild landscapes survive only as enclaves in a matrix of human dominion. These enclaves are so few, so starkly demarcated, that we label them individually — with names like Yosemite, Bob Marshall, Serengeti, Royal Chitwan, Arctic National Wildlife Refuge. The next stage will be that we abolish nature utterly; or that we restrain ourselves uncharacteristically; or that we bring favored bits of it indoors, to be pampered and possessed as biological knickknacks, nearly meaningless in their disconnection from context.

The California condor, for instance, has already been taken indoors. The black-footed ferret is indoors. Martha, the last passenger pigeon, died indoors at the Cincinnati Zoo. *Leucopsar rothschildi* sheds light on this stage of history, because it too seems destined for a future as small as indoors.

Leucopsar rothschildi is the world's most beautiful and endangered starling.

This one is a looking-glass story, everything backwards. Out is in, down is up, bad is good, and the starling in question is a precious bird of stunning white plumage. Its eyes are set off by a mask of naked blue skin. It wears a long feathery crest off the back of its head, erected at will when it wants to impress a potential mate. It's desperately rare but also common, a paradox reflecting the paradoxical notion that nature can be taken indoors: As a wild animal, it's rare; as an inmate of zoos, common. In the wild state, which is now mainly a state of memory, *Leucopsar rothschildi* occupied a thin strip of dry forest along the northwestern coast of the island of Bali, in Indonesia. Its range has shrunk as the population of birds has shrunk, though on the extreme northwestern nub of the island a relatively few survivors remain. It's endemic to Bali — meaning, native to non of the other 13,000 Indonesian islands — and in fact it's Bali's only endemic bird. Why this unique species should appear just on Bali, a small island, a young island, is a mystery.

It changes names like a genie changes shape. To the Indonesian people it's know as *jalak putih* — and *putih* seems to carry the sense of "immaculate" as well as "white." So the bird can be taken for a symbol of purity, an ideal of the pristine, as well as an emblem of the spectacular biological riches encompassed by this great archipelago of a country. In the English-speaking world, some folks have been pleased to fancy it up as "Rothschild's mynah." "Starling" is an unsavory word to American ornithologists in particular, and for good historical reasons: *Sturnus vulgaris*, the European starling, in the century since it was introduced here, has flourished malignly as one of America's most successful and unwelcome species. "Mynah" sounds more singular and tropical. "Mynah" suggests a magical talent for speech. But a spade is a spade and *Leucopsar rothschildi*, among the bird experts I've talked with in Indonesia, is simply the Bali starling.

It tolerates captivity well — probably too well for its own good. During the early 1960s, *Leucopsar rothschildi* suffered a plague of popularity among private bird-breeders. Hundred of Bali starlings were exported from Indonesia to these American and European aviculturists, who either didn't know or didn't care that the species was already scarce in the wild. Mercenary bird-catchers, working the Balinese forest with nets and with birdlime (a sticky substance, spread on branches to serve as the avian equivalent of flypaper), were happy to meet the demand. In those years, commercial trapping of *Leucopsar rothschildi* was still legal. Indonesian customers supported a share of the trade too, indulging their love of caged birds as a traditional form of decor. Among some of the more affluent collectors, especially in Bali and Java, a *jalak putih* was a prized item. Then, in 1971, a new Indonesian law decreed the species protected against hunting, capture, and export. But to decree protection is not to effect it, and the bird-catchers continued to operate. Even the establishment of Bali Barat National Park, encompassing most of the bird's range, hasn't shut off the trade. A Bali starling may now be worth as much as $300 on the black market, so the incentive is high. These poachers are well financed, well equipped, and stealthy; some even come in on bird-catching raids, by boat, from the island of Java. The park guards, in contrast, have been chronically short of the resources needed for enforcement. The guards have no guns and only occasional use of a boat. They spend days at a stretch camped at bleak guard-stations around the seacoast perimeter of the park, living on rice, dried fish, and fresh water stored there in carboys. They play chess by lantern to fill the long evenings, and at daylight they walk out on patrol. They do what they can.

Anyway, poaching is only half the problem. There's also been an inexorable trend of habitat loss with Bali's crowded and hungry human population converting ever more of the northwestern forest into firewood, coconut plantation, cropland, and villages.

Back in 1966, because of these factors, the International Union for Conversation of Nature and Natural Resources listed the species as endangered. That listing seems to have incited zoos in the West, with the best of motives, to get into the business of breeding *Leucopsar rothschildi*. The zoo people all knew it was rare, beautiful, failing, so the prospect of a captive-bred population must have seemed both tantalizing and constructive. Endangered species are good box-office at zoos, and of course captive breeding, if done with the proper concern for genetic diversity and pedigree records, can be a crucial part of a larger conversation strategy. In those years, for the starling, there was no larger strategy. There was simply a vague sense that — who knows? — maybe captive-bred birds would turn out to be a last hedge against total extinction. So a number of farsighted zoos each took in a pair or two of *Leucopsar rothschildi*, and from those few birds were bred many. For one instance, the Jersey Wildlife Preservation Trust (Gerald Durrell's organization, a leader in species-rescue efforts) acquired four Bali starlings in 1971, and within the next two decades the JWPT had reared at least 185. The captive-bred population throughout Europe and America included hundreds more. Unfortunately, genetic diversity and pedigree records didn't always get the attention they deserved. Some institutions simply produced an abundance of inbred starlings. Some couldn't recall whether their birds were inbred or not. "By the early 1980s the zoo population in North America had multiplied to nearly 500," according to Don Bruning, head of the ornithology department at the New York Zoological Society. "The zoos were saturated with bird." A sad irony of that situation, in Bruning's view, was that legal restrictions related to officially "endangered" status discouraged the moving of birds from one zoo to another, which otherwise could have mitigated inbreeding. Don Bruning has probably worked on behalf of *Leucopsar rothschildi* as long and as fervently as anyone. Two years ago, by his estimate, the world-wide zoo population stood at more than 1,000. In the wild, he guessed, only 60 to 70 Bali starlings survived.

By the time I reached northwestern Bali in the spring of last year, the wild population was less than 30.

I rode out to an isolated stretch of that Balinese coastline, within sight of the volcanoes of Java, on board a sputtering old gray boat. I was tagging along with a contingent of park guards and the two field officers in charge of the bird project, an Indonesian named M. Noor Soetawidjaya and a transplanted Dutchman named Bas van Balen. At an outpost called Teluk Kelor, we went ashore. The guard station had a concrete floor, plank bunks, an unobtrusive population of geckos and rats, and walls of thatched rattan, on one of which hung a faded poster. Here was the gorgeous white bird itself, in a glossy photo. The caption below was in Indonesian, but Bas translated: "Bali Starling — once extinct, it won't ever be created again." We shared the guards' dried fish and rice, and kibitzed their lantern-lit chess. Early the next morning, scanning the treetops with binoculars from a hillside nearby, under the guidance of Bas, I saw four Bali starlings. It was more than a tenth of the world's wild population at that moment.

I also saw the marks left by a party of poachers who had gotten away clean just a few weeks before. I saw a small broken twig, to which a single white feather was glued with birdlime. And now, a year later, according to the latest field census report from Bass and Noor, which has reached me by fax, there seem to be no more than 18 birds left. Possibly as few as 13.

Despite efforts to protect it, such a tiny population could easily disappear within the next year or two. One poaching raid could cut it in half. One hurricane, one viral disease, could kill 18 birds at a stroke. It could happen almost faster than fax.

The zoos are still full of *Leucopsar rothschildi*. So by the narrowest of and most reductionist sense in which we contemplate the ontology of a species, this species won't soon be extinct. But in a less reductionist sense, the Bali starling is desperately close to its end. It's a wild animal facing the sad and immediate possibility of becoming a biological knickknack.

The end may be near but it isn't inevitable. There's a glimmer or two of good news amid the bad, and there's a window of hope. In April of last year, 13 captive-bred birds were released into the wild. By December, at least one of those former captives had paired with a wild bird. Not long ago, according to Bas van Balen, that pair successfully fledged three chicks. It's a small event. But the future of *Leucopsar rothschildi* depends on an aggregation of such small events.

The current program to rescue the Bali starling, launched in 1987, is a collaboration among four bodies: the Indonesian directorate charged with nature conservation (PHPA), the American Association of Zoological Parks and Aquariums (AAZPA), Durrell's JWPT, and the British-based International Council for Bird Preservation (ICBP). The immediate goals sound simple: Stop poaching, prevent further loss of habitat, and put as many captive-bred birds as possible back into the wild. Each is less simple than it sounds. The Indonesian PHPA and the ICBP together oversee the monitoring and (attempted) protection of the birds in the wild. The AAZPA takes responsibility for operating a Pre-Release Training Center — a small building with a few attached cages, near the habitat site in Bali Barat National Park, where select captive-bred starlings are given conditioning intended to help them survive on their own. In consultation with both the AAZPA and the JWPT, the Indonesian PHPA also supervises a special breeding facility at a zoo in the city of Surabaya, on the island of Java. The birds that go back into the wild are chosen from among those hatched at Surabaya. The founder stock, taken there in 1987, consisted of 39 starlings from American zoos and four from the JWPT all carefully chosen on the basis of pedigree records so that inbreeding could be minimized. Other breeding stock will be added as appropriate birds become available. The fewer generations spent in captivity, the more promising a particular lineage is likely to be. Therefore, the wild birds that poachers have recently taken, if any such birds can be found and acquired, are especially precious at Surabaya. But with *Leucopsar rothschildi* now a protected species in Indonesia, the people who buy from the poachers tend to keep quiet. So the government has instituted a "white-wash campaign," an ingenious offer to the owners of black-market starlings that they can legalize their ownership by trading a poacher-caught bird for a captive-bred bird from an American zoo. The poacher-caught birds are genetically preferable for the breeding project at Surabaya, whereas the birds whose parents and grandparents and great-grandparents were captive-bred creatures are probably better adapted to survive as decor. Suddenly there's a good use for some of those inbred, indoorsy zoo animals. Down is up, out is in, black is white.

The most complicated component of this whole effort — scientifically, if not politically — is the breeding, rearing, selection, transport, and training of birds for release to the wild. But the political dimension is also complicated and crucial. Genetic analysis, bird husbandry, dedicated guards, and restoration ecology are not enough to save *Leucopsar rothschildi*. Political will is also necessary. And lately there's some encouraging news in this area too.

The whitewash campaign has turned up at least 40 wild-caught birds in the vicinity of Jakarta. The governor of Bali has reportedly agreed to a plan that will translocate one village (an enclave, within the enclave that is Bali Barat National Park, within the enclave of land that is Bali) from inside to outside the park boundary. A new chief of the park has been appointed, with a strong mandate from his government to strengthen the guard's position and finally shut off the poaching. Maybe it isn't too late.

Indonesia is a big country, spread out across 3,000 miles of tropical ocean, from a point west of Singapore to a point east of Darwin. It encompasses more human cultures, more languages, than Europe. It includes the islands of Sumatra, Java, most of Borneo, Sulawesi, Timor, Komodo, Flores, Seram, the Moluccas, the western half of New Guinea, Lombok, Bali, and about 12,990 others. In terms of biological richness, it's probably the second most significant nation on earth, surpassed only by Brazil. It harbors the last wild population of Javan rhinoceros. The last wild population of Sumatran tiger. A sizable portion of the last wild orangutans. It harbors spiral-tusked pigs on Sulawesi, birds of paradise on New Guinea, giant monitor lizards on Komodo, proboscis monkeys on Borneo. Like most tropical countries, of course, Indonesia presently faces dire problems and difficult choices related to human population, hunger, resource exploitation, and settlement, as well as a scowl of international pressure to avoid making precisely the same sort of mistake by which we Americans have destroyed our wolves, our hardwood forests, and 60 million bison. Maybe the Indonesian people and their government can find a breadth of vision, and a political will, somewhat larger than ours. But unlike geography those things can't be directly measured.

Indonesia harbors pangolins, cassowaries, cockatoos, and cuscuses. It harbors tree kangaroos. It harbors birdwing butterflies seven inches across. It harbors lorises, lories, and lorikeets. Tarsiers, sambar deer, moon rats, sun bears, bantengs, bandicoots, colugos, siamangs, too many other treasures to list or to count. It's an astonishing and important place. On the island of Bali, by the time you read this, there may or may not be a wondrous white starling.

Intimate Relations and the Extinction of Experience

by Robert Michael Pyle

*"Everywhere desire to restore and nowhere demand; surfeit of world,
and earth enough."*
— Rainer Maria Rilke, *Holding Out*

I became a nonbeliever and a conservationist in one fell swoop. All it took
was the Lutherans paving their parking lot.

The central, unavoidable fact of my childhood was the public school system of Aurora, Colorado. My path to school for ten out of twelve years followed the same route: down Revere Street, left at the fire hall, along Hoffman
Park to Del Mar Circle; then around the Circle to Peoria Street, and on to
whichever school was currently claiming my time. Detours occurred regularly, according to opportunity and curiosity.

The intersection of Hoffman Boulevard and Peoria Street was two corners sacred, two profane. On the southeast squatted the white-brick Baptist
church. Across Del Mar lay a vacant lot full of pigweed, where my brother
and I cached brown bananas and other cast-offs foraged from behind Busley's
Supermarket, in case we might need provisions on some future expedition.
Then came the Phillips 66 gas station and the Kwik Shake, a 19-cent ham-
burger stand whose jukebox played "Peggy Sue" if you so much as looked at
it and tossed a nickel in its direction. And on the northeast corner lay the
red-brick lair of the Lutherans, marginally modern, with a stained-glass cross
in the wall. I spent quite a lot of time dawdling in the vacant lot among the

pigweed and haunting the Kwik Shake after school, but I seldom loitered in the precincts of the church-goers.

Lukewarm Methodists at best, my parents flipped a coin and took us to the Lutheran service for Easter. The next Christmas I was roped in to being a Wise Man, and I felt both silly and cold in my terry-cloth robe. Later, when my great-grandmother came from Toledo to live with us, she hauled me off Sundays to the Southern Baptists. Gimma desperately wanted me to go down the aisle and be saved. A shy boy, I wasn't about to prostrate myself in public before a bunch of people with big smiles and bad grammar. Besides, I couldn't see the sense in confessing to sins I didn't feel I had properly enjoyed as yet. Had I been compelled to choose among them, I'd have taken the cool, impersonal approach of the Lutherans over the Baptists' warmhearted but embarrassing bear-hug of a welcome. But Gimma passed on, and my parents pushed in neither direction, so I opted for the corporeal pleasures of "Peggy Sue" and pigweed and put the soul on hold.

Behind the Lutheran Church lay another, smaller vacant lot, where the congregation parked in the mud. The new community of Hoffman Heights had been built partly on a filled-in lake. The water poked up here and there, making marshy spots full of plants that grew nowhere else around, like cattails and curly dock. The far corner of the Lutherans' lot held one of the last of these.

One September day coming home from school I cut across the boggy corner, almost dried out with late summer and tall with weeds. Pink knotweed daubed the broken mud and scented the afternoon air. Then I noticed, fully spread on the knotweed bloom, a butterfly. It was more than an inch across, richly brown like last year's pennies, with a purple sheen when the sun caught it just right. I knelt and watched it for a long time. There were others flitting around, some of them orange, some brown, but this one stayed put, basking. Then a car drove by, disturbing it. The last thing I noticed before it flew was a broad, bright zig-zag of fire-engine orange across its hind wings.

A couple of years later, when I became an ardent collector, I remembered the butterfly in the Del Mar marshlet clearly. My Peterson field guide showed me that it was, without question, a bronze copper. The orangey ones had been females. Professor Klots wrote that it is "the largest of our coppery Coppers" and "Not uncommon, but quite local. Seek a colony," he wrote, "in open, wet meadows." Dr Brown, in my bible, *Colorado Butterflies*, explained that the species extended no farther west than the plains of eastern Colorado, and called it *very* local (which I translated as "rare"). He went on to say that "the best places to seek (*Lycaena*) *thoe* in Colorado are the weedy borders of well-established reservoirs on the plains," which the Hoffman Heights lake had certainly been. Eagerly I prepared to return to the spot at the right time and obtain *Lycaena thoe* for my collection.

Then, in early summer, the Lutherans pulled their fell swoop: they paved the parking lot. In the process they dumped loads of broken concrete and earth fill into the little marsh, obliterating it, and covered it with thick black asphalt. Gone were the curly docks, the knotweeds, the coppers. Searching all around Aurora over the next few years I failed to find another colony, nor even a single bronze copper. That was the first extinction, if only local, that I was to witness. Many more followed. The field in which I later threw discus obliterated the habitat of the Olympia marblewing, and a miniature golf course wiped out the only colony of brilliant goatweed emperors in the district. Innocence was lost.

I decided that I would do what I could to prevent travesties like these when I grew up. I also concluded that a good and loving god would never permit his faithful servants to do such a thing, and gave up on the Lutherans and their like for the long run.

Biologists agree that the rate of species extinction has risen sharply since the introduction of agriculture and industry to the human landscape. Soon, the decline might mirror ancient mass extinction episodes that were caused by atmospheric or astronomic events. In response, we compile lists and redbooks of endangered species, and seek to manage conditions in their favor. This is good, if only occasionally successful in dramatic terms.

Our concern for the absolute extinction of species is highly appropriate. As our partners in earth's enterprise drop out, we find ourselves lonelier, less sure of our ability to hold together the tattered business of life. Every effort to prevent further losses is worthwhile, no matter how disruptive, for diversity is its own reward. But outright extinction is not the only problem. By concentrating on the truly rare and endangered plants and animals, conservation efforts often neglect another form of loss that can have striking consequences: the local extinction.

Protection almost always focuses on rarity as the criterion for attention. Conservation ecologists employ a whole lexicon of categories to define scarceness. In ascending order of jeopardy, the hierarchy usually includes the terms "of concern" (="monitor"), "sensitive," "threatened (="vulnerable"), and "endangered." All types so listed might fairly be called "rare." But people tend to employ that term when some other word might be better.

Most species listed as endangered are genuinely rare in the absolute sense: their range is highly restricted and their total number is never very high. Biologists recognize a fuzzy threshold below which the populations of these organisms should not drop, lest their extinction likely follow. That level is a kind of critical mass, the minimum number necessary to maintain mating and other essential functions. A creature is profoundly rare when its members are so few as to approach this perilous line.

But often, perceived rarity is a matter of the relative distribution of a species over time and space. The monarch butterfly, for example, is virtually absent from the Maritime Northwest due to the absence of milkweed; while across most of North America, it is considered a commonplace creature. Patchy and fluctuating from year to year when dispersed in the summertime, monarchs become incredibly abundant in their Mexican and Californian winter roosts. Yet the migration of the North American monarch is listed as an "endangered phenomenon" due to the extreme vulnerability of the winter clusters.

Another range-and-black butterfly, the painted lady, appears in the North by the millions from time to time. In certain springs, such as that of 1991, these butterflies block entire highways with their very numbers. In drier years, when their southern winter habitat produces little nectar, nary a lady might be seen in the temperate regions come summertime. Nevertheless, this thistle-loving immigrant is so widespread globally that its alternate name is the cosmopolite. What are we to make of such patterns? Are these insects common, or rare? Evidently they can be either. Painted ladies and monarchs stretch our sense of the word "rare."

The concept becomes a little less slippery when we speak of sedentary or specialized animals and plants such as the bronze copper. But are such creatures actually rare, or merely "local," as Professor Klots described the copper in 1951? The fact is that as the countryside condenses under human influence, that which was only local has a way of becoming genuinely scarce. Somewhere along the continuum from abundance to extinction, a passenger pigeon becomes a pileated woodpecker, then a northern spotted owl, and then nothing at all.

In light of the relativity of rarity, it is not surprising that scarce wildlife preservation resources go almost entirely to the more truly rare species. But, as with Ronald Reagan's decision to restrict federal aid to those he considered "truly needy," this practice leaves many vulnerable populations subject to extinction at the local level.

Local extinctions matter, for at least three major reasons. First, evolutionary biologists know that natural selection operates intensely on "edge" populations. This is known as the Sewell Wright effect, after the biologist who detected that the cutting edge of evolution might be the extremities of a species' range rather than the center, where it is more numerous. Local extinctions commonly occur on the edges, depriving species of this important opportunity for adaptive change.

Second, little losses add up to big losses. A colony goes extinct here, a population drops out there — and before you know it, you have an endangered species. Attrition, once under way, is progressive. "Between German chickens and Irish hogs," wrote San Francisco entomologist H.H. Behr to his Chicago friend Herman Strecker in 1875, "no insect can exist besides louse and flea." Behr was lamenting the diminution of native insects on the San Francisco Peninsula. Already at that early date, butterflies such as the Xerces blue were becoming difficult to find, as colony after colony disappeared before the expanding city. In the early 1940s the Xerces blue became absolutely extinct. Local extinctions accumulate, amounting to a drastically undermined flora and fauna.

The third consequence of local loss involves another kind of depletion altogether. I call it *the extinction of experience*. Simply stated, the loss of neighborhood species endangers our experience of nature. If a species becomes extinct within our own radius of reach (smaller for the very old, very young, disabled, and poor), it might as well be gone altogether, in one important sense. To those whose access suffers by it, local extinction has much the same result as global eradication.

Of course we are all diminished by the extirpation of animals and plants wherever they occur. Many people take deep satisfaction in wilderness and wildlife they will never see. But direct, personal contact with other living things affects us in vital ways that vicarious experience can never replace.

I believe that one of the greatest causes of the ecological crisis is the state of personal alienation from nature in which many people live. We lack a widespread sense of intimacy with the living world. Natural history has never been more popular in some ways, yet few people organize their lives around nature, or even allow it to affect them profoundly. Our depth of contact is too often wanting. Two distinctive birds, by the ways in which they fish, furnish a model for what I mean.

Brown pelicans fish by slamming directly into the sea, great bills agape, making sure of solid contact with the resource they seek. Black skimmers, graceful, tern-like birds with longer lower mandibles than upper, fly over the surface with just the lower half of their bills in the water. They catch fish too, but avoid bodily immersion by merely skimming the surface.

In my view, most people who consider themselves nature lovers behave more like skimmers than pelicans. They buy the right outfits at L.L. Bean and Eddie Bauer, carry field guides, and take walks on nature trails, reading all the interpretive signs. They watch the nature programs on television, shop at The Nature Company, and pay their dues to the National Wildlife Federation or the National Audubon Society. Their activities are admirable, but they seldom make truly intimate contact with nature. Instead they skim, reaping a shallow reward. And these are the exceptional ones — the great majority of the people associate with nature even less.

When the natural world becomes chiefly an entertainment or a diversion for the affluent, it loses its ability to arouse our deeper instincts. Professor E.O. Wilson of Harvard University, winner of two Pulitzer Prizes for his penetrating looks at both humans and insects, believes we all possess a capacity for what he calls "biophilia." To Wilson, this means that humans have an innate desire to connect with other life forms, and that to do so is highly salutary. Nature is therapeutic. As short-story writer Valerie Martin tells us in "The Consolation of Nature," only nature can restore a sense of safety in the end. So where does the courtship fail? How can we engage our biophilia?

Everyone has at least a chance of realizing a pleasurable and collegial wholeness with nature. But to get there, intimate association is necessary. A banana slug, face-to-face, means much more than a Komodo dragon seen on television. With rhinos mating in the living room, who will care about the creatures next door? At least the skimmers are aware of nature. As for the others, for whom nature has little place in their lives, how can they even care at all?

The extinction of experience is not just about losing the personal benefits of the natural high. It also implies a cycle of disaffection that can have disastrous consequences. As cities and metastasizing suburbs forsake their natural diversity, and their citizens grow more removed from personal contact with nature, awareness and appreciation retreat. This breeds apathy toward environmental concerns and, inevitably, further degradation of the common habitat.

So it goes, on and on, the extinction of experience sucking the life from the land, the intimacy from our connections. This is how the passing of otherwise common species from our immediate vicinities can be as significant as the total loss of rarities. People who care, conserve; people who don't know, don't care. What is the extinction of the condor to a child who has never known a wren?

In teaching about butterflies, I will often place a living butterfly on a child's nose. Noses seem to make perfectly good perches or basking spots, and the insect will often remain for some time. Almost everyone is delighted by this, the light tickle, the close-up colors, the thread of a tongue probing for droplets of perspiration. But somewhere beyond delight lies enlightenment. I have been astonished at the small epiphanies I see in the eyes of a child in truly close contact with nature, perhaps for the first time. This can happen to grown-ups too, reminding them of something they never knew they had forgotten.

We are finally discovering the link between our biophilia and our future. With new eyes, planners are leaving nature in the suburbs and inviting it back into the cities as never before. For many species the effort comes too late, since once gone, they can be desperately difficult to re-establish. But at least the adaptable types can be fostered with care and forethought.

The initiatives of urban ecologists are making themselves felt in many cities. In Portland, Oregon, Urban Naturalist Mike Houck worked to have the great blue heron designated the official city bird, to have a local micro-brewery fashion an ale to commemorate it, and to fill in the green-leaks in a forty-mile loop greenway envisioned decades ago. Now known as the "140-Mile Loop," it ties in with a massive urban greenspaces program on both sides of the Columbia River. An international conference entitled "Country in the City" takes place annually in Portland, pushing urban diversity. These kinds of efforts arise from a recognition of the extinction of experience, and a fervid desire to avoid its consequences.

Lately, Mike Houck has launched an effort to involve the arts community in refreshing the cities, and devoted himself to urban stream restoration. This practice has led to one of the few nouns-into-verbs of which I wholeheartedly approve: streams rescued from the storm-drains are said to be "daylighted" — a delightful term. When each city has someone like Mike Houck working to daylight its streams, save its woods, and educate its planners, the sources of our experience will be safer.

But nature reserves and formal greenways are not enough to ensure connection. Such places, important as they are, invite a measured, restricted kind of contact. When children come along with an embryonic interest in natural history, they need free places for pottering, netting, catching, and watching.

67

Insects, crawdads, and tadpoles can stand to be nabbed a good deal. This has always been the usual route to a serious interest in biology. To expect a strictly appreciative response from a child at first is quixotic. Young naturalists need the "trophy," hands-on stage before leap-frogging on to mere looking. There need to be places that are not kid-proofed, where children can do damage, and come back next year to see the results.

Likewise, we all need spots near home where we can wander off a trail, lift a stone, poke about, and merely wonder: places where no interpretive signs intrude their message to rob our spontaneous response. Along with the nature centers, parks, and preserves, we would do well to maintain a modicum of open space with no rule but common courtesy, no sign besides animal tracks.

For these purposes, nothing serves better than the hand-me-down habitats that lie somewhere between formal protection and development. Throwaway landscapes like this used to occur on the edges of settlement everywhere. Richard Mabey, a British writer and naturalist, describes them as the "unofficial countryside." He speaks of ignominious, degraded, forgotten places that we have discarded, serving nonetheless as habitats for an array of plants and animals: derelict railway land, ditchbanks, abandoned farms or bankrupt building sites, old gravel pits and factory yards, embankments, margins of landfills. These are the survivors, the colonizers, the generalists — the so-called weedy species. Or, in secreted corners and remnants of older habitat types — like the Lutherans' parking lot — specialists and rarities may remain to be discovered. Developers, realtors, and the common parlance refer to such weedy enclaves as "vacant lots" and "waste ground." But these are two of my favorite oxymorons: what, to a curious kid, is less vacant than a vacant lot? Less waste than waste ground?

I grew up in a landscape lavishly scattered with unofficial countryside — vacant lots aplenty, a neglected so-called park where weeds had their way, yesterday's farms, and the endless open ground of an old irrigation ditch called the High Line Canal looping off east and west. These were the leftovers of the early suburban leap. They were rich with possibility. I could catch a bug, grab a crawdad, run screaming from a giant garden spider: intimacy abounded.

But Aurora slathered itself across the High Plains, its so-called city limits becoming broader than those of Denver itself. In reality it knew no limits — neither the limit of available water, nor that of livability. Of course the lots filled in, losing the legacy of their vacancy. The park actually became one, and almost all of its fascination fled before the spade and the blade of the landscaper's art. And by the time the canal became an official pathway, part of the National Trail System, most of the little nodes of habitat in its curves and loops were long gone. The experience I'd known was buried in the 'burbs.

On a recent visit, I watched many more kids walking along the canal than in my day. But there was so much less to see. No one seemed to be catching bugs, nabbing crawdads, or running from spiders. Merely putting people and nature together does not insure intimacy; to these kids, the canal path might have meant little more than a loopy sidewalk. But I wondered, if any of them were inclined to look, would there be anything left to find?

The next day I followed the High Line Canal out onto the plains. A few dozen tall cottonwoods marked off a remnant stretch strung between a freeway and a new town. Where the ditch dove into a culvert beneath a road, an old marshy margin survived. Monarchs sailed from milkweed to goldenrod. Then I spotted a smaller brilliancy among the fall flowers. Netting it, I found it was a bronze copper — the first I'd seen in more than thirty years, since the Lutherans paved their parking lot. There were others. Houses were going in nearby. Maybe, I thought, releasing it, some kid with a Peterson field guide would happen across this little colony before the end of it.

Had it not been for the High Line Canal, the vacant lots I knew, the scruffy park, I'm not at all certain I would have become a biologist. I might have been a lawyer, or even a Lutheran. The total immersion in nature that I found in those places was a baptism of faith that never wavered, but it was a matter of happenstance too. It was the place that made me.

How many people grow up with such windows on the world? Fewer and fewer, I fear, as metropolitan habitats disappear and rural ones blend into the urban fringe. The number of people living in monotony, with little hint of nature in their lives, is very large and growing. This isn't good for us. To gain the solace of nature, we need to connect deeply. Few ever do.

In the long run, this mass estrangement from things natural bodes ill for countryside conservation and the care of the earth. If we are to forge new links to the land, we must resist the extinction of experience. We must save the vacant lots, the ditches, and the woodlots, along with the old growth. We must become believers in the world.

DEATH AND RESURRECTION:

THE REbIRTH of SpIRIT LAKE

by DouglAs W. LARSON

There are rare instances in which a lake appears to be dead, but miraculously recovers and, temporarily at least, delays its inevitable extinction. One such lake was Spirit Lake, located at the base of Mount St. Helens in Washington, about five miles north of the mountain's renowned conical peak.

Actually, Spirit Lake owed its existence to Mount St. Helens, which had blocked the upper Toutle River valley with volcanic deposits many centuries ago. This volcanic dam impounded the headwaters of the North Fork of the Toutle River, creating a lake which, according to an ancient Indian legend, harbored "a demon so huge that its hand could stretch across the entire lake." Indians who were foolish enough to visit and fish Spirit Lake, so the story went, were certain to be grabbed by the demon's monstrous hand and pulled to the lake's fathomless depths. White humans, chiefly of European descent, pooh-poohed the Indians' long-standing fear of Spirit Lake monsters and defiantly exploited the lake for their summertime recreation, establishing a hodgepodge of cabins, lodges, campgrounds, and boating docks along the shoreline.

In 1980, slowly awakening to this disregard for sacred realms, the demon suddenly uncorked its top and spewed death and destruction across the May time waters of Spirit Lake. A few days later, a small contingent of scientists sent to Mount St. Helens took one look at Spirit Lake and pronounced it dead.

Lakes, created by inexorable and often violent forces of nature, are fated for extinction as they evolve from youthful to mature to senescent bodies of water. The evolution of a lake — lasting for thousands of years in some cases and only a few decades in others — follows a continuous and usually irreversible course. Throughout this evolutionary process the lake gradually fills with a mixture of natural materials washed in from the surrounding watershed — primarily soils, minerals, and organic debris — and with vegetation produced within the lake itself. Ultimately, a lacustrine plain, underlain by distinctive layers of mostly silt, clay, and organic deposits, marks the site of an extinct lake.

Newborn lakes appear in the aftermath of epic periods of geological restlessness. Glaciers, volcanoes, earthquakes, mountainous landslides, erosive rivers, wind-blown sands, and continental rifting are the preeminent means of lake formation. This geological unrest, either prolonged or abrupt, creates the basins that will eventually capture and contain primordial lakewaters.

Life in pristine lakes is primitive and sparse, if it exists at all, owing to the meagerness of essential nutritive elements such as nitrogen and phosphorus. As time passes, however, a wide variety of specialized aquatic life forms take up residence, including bacteria, protozoans, microscopic algae (phytoplankton), microscopic animals (zooplankton), bottom-dwelling algae (periphyton), rooted aquatic plants (macrophytes), insects, fish, and amphibians. Plants, the primary producers in this highly complex biological assemblage, photosysthetically convert solar radiation to organic matter which sustains higher organisms in the lake's food chain. But aquatic plants may overproduce in response to increasing lakewater fertility prompted by nutrient-bearing pollutants entering the lake. The end result of excessive nutrient enrichment is an overabundance of vegetation which infests the entire lake and, consequently, accelerates the evolutionary, or lake-aging, process. A lake is said to be dying when its original basin is nearly filled with sludge-like deposits capped by luxuriant growths of vegetation that may cover much, if not all, of the lake's surface. Death, a peat bog, is now close at hand. Dry land finally succeeds deep waters. Certainly lake extinction.

The catastrophic volcanic eruption of Mount St. Helens on May 18, 1980 devastated vast forestlands, triggered massive landslides and mudflows, and filled several nearby lakes with timber and volcanic debris.

The largest of the lakes impacted was Spirit Lake, positioned north of the exploding volcano at an elevation of 3,200 feet. What had been a largely unspoiled, relatively large (two miles square in area and 185 feet deep), alpine lake was reduced within minutes to a roiling, steaming body of water choked with logs and mud.

Spirit Lake received enormous quantities of debris avalanche materials, tens of thousands of trees, cremated forest vegetation, and minerals of magmatic and lithic origin. Incoming volcanic debris was sufficient in quantity to displace the lake's surface elevation upward by about 200 feet over the pre-eruption level. The sum effect of this deposition was to produce a shallower, expanded basin, with its storage capacity reduced by 10 percent from pre-eruption conditions.

This volcanic influx greatly increased lakewater concentrations of inorganic chemical constituents, as well as dissolved and particulate organic matter: the lake's post-eruption concentrations of iron and manganese were, respectively, more than 5000 times and 1000 times higher than pre-eruption amounts. The concentration of total organic carbon rose from 1.3 milligrams per liter (pre-eruption) to 41 milligrams per liter after the eruption.

Much of the deposited organic matter was incorporated in the lake's new sediment layer, which was 150 to 200 feet thick. The lake was also a depository for high-temperature pyroclastic flows and mudflows, ashfall, and geothermal waters, which increased lakewater temperatures to 90 degrees Fahrenheit and possibly higher.

Unusually warm lakewaters, acting in concert with the massive inorganic (iron, manganese, and other metals) and organic loadings to Spirit Lake, prompted the lake's bacteria to proliferate rapidly. Within a month of the eruption, bacteria in shallow waters numbered close to one-half billion cells per milliliter, a density thought to be unprecedented in the annals of microbiology. The bacteria proceeded to decompose and oxidize orogenic matter found abundantly in lakewaters and lake sediments. This process soon exhausted the lake's supply of oxygen, allowing only anaerobic microorganisms to survive in the lake during the summer and fall of 1980 when lake-degradation was most severe.

The fate of other biological components of the lake's pre-eruption ecosystem, such as protozoans, algae, rooted plants, zooplankton, insects, fish, and amphibians is poorly known. It was speculated that most of the plants and animals in Spirit Lake were simply buried by the overwhelming deluge of volcanic deposits. Fish and other oxygen-requiring organisms that happened to survive this initial impact were killed shortly by the abrupt loss of oxygen (consumed entirely by bacteria) and perhaps by toxic compounds that were building in the lake.

Plant life in Spirit Lake essentially disappeared after the eruption. Only a few remnant phytoplankton cells were collected from the lake during the summer and fall of 1980. The elimination of green plants in Spirit Lake, including the phytoplankton, periphyton, and macrophytes, effectively halted photosynthetic activity. Consequently, the lake's ecosystem was no longer being fueled by solar energy captured and stored by aquatic plant life. Instead, for two years after the 1980 eruption of Mount St. Helens, organic matter in Spirit Lake was synthesized almost entirely by specialized bacteria called chemotrophs. These microbes converted the lake's tremendous load of inorganic chemicals — particularly iron, manganese, sulfur, and nitrogen — from one form to another, thereby releasing energy chemosynthetically for other biological functions.

Further indications of extreme water-quality degradation in Spirit Lake included: (1) powerful generation of hazardous gases in lakewater and lake-bottom sediments, principally methane and hydrogen sulfide; (2) the abundance of various toxic organic compounds such as phenols; (3) large concentrations of potentially toxic metals, including arsenic, lead, mercury, and cadmium; and (4) opaque, blackish-looking lakewaters resulting from prodigious organic decomposition and sulfur enrichment. Additionally, and perhaps most ominous, the lake was highly contaminated with several types of pathogenic bacteria, notably *Legionella* bacteria which causes the sometimes-fatal Legionnaires' disease. Indeed, Spirit Lake appeared to be dead and lifeless, except for the astronomical numbers of bacteria feeding on the carcass.

Despite reports from the field and elsewhere indicating that Spirit Lake was dead, limnologists (lake scientists) were inclined to believe that the old body of water still had a pulse. These scientists realized, of course, that the entire Spirit Lake basin, and all of its surrounding watershed, had been radically and irreversibly altered by the mountain's cataclysmic eruption. But they hypothesized nevertheless that the lake's hugely deteriorated condition would eventually improve, that the lake would be recolonized by plants and animals, and that a more "typical" lake ecosystem would again prevail. Scientists, assuming that Spirit Lake would probably recover, were excited by the once-in-a-lifetime opportunity to study firsthand the natural restoration of a large aquatic ecosystem that had been suddenly and totally destroyed.

What scientists wanted to learn from the Spirit Lake disaster was how long the lake's recovery would take and what would be the nature of the "recovered" ecosystem. They predicted, as all reputable scientists must, that Spirit Lake's recovery — vaguely defined as the return to pre-eruption chemical and biological conditions — would require 10-20 years and perhaps longer.

Between 1980 and 1989, limnologists and other scientists made over 100 helicopter-borne field trips into the Mount St. Helens blast zone to scientifically document the predicted recovery of Spirit Lake. The results were astonishing. The scientists reported the following: (1) the quality of the lake had improved markedly by 1986, with the greatest improvement occurring between 1980 and 1982; (2) by 1981, much of the lake had become saturated with oxygen year-round, indicating that organic matter and other oxygen-consuming agents had diminished considerably in quantity and strength; (3) concentrations of most lakewater chemicals, notably iron and manganese, had decreased significantly by 1986, some falling close to pre-eruption levels; (4) the numbers of bacteria recorded in 1986 were back to normal levels, at least a thousand times fewer than the numbers reported shortly after the 1980 eruption; (5) the clarity, or transparency, of the lake had increased to such an extent that sunlight during the summer of 1986 reached depths of 60-70 feet, similar to pre-eruption sunlight penetration; (6) the lake's phytoplankton community was reestablished by 1986 (the number of phytoplankton species increased from fewer than 20 in summer 1980 to 135 in 1986), primarily because of improved lakewater clarity and water quality; (7) phytoplankton photosynthesis during 1986 and after had all but replaced bacterial chemosynthesis as the principal means of obtaining energy for biological growth and production; and (8) logs and other forest debris, hurled into the lake during the 1980 eruption, continued to form a giant raft covering much of the lake in 1989.

Recently, scientists have discovered that portions of Spirit Lake are filling in with rooted aquatic plants, or macrophytes. The south end of the lake, in particular, is now heavily vegetated. This area still receives warm, chemically enriched geothermal seepwaters from the debris avalanche at the base of Mount St. Helens. The south end of the lake is also shoaled by organically laden, chemically rich muds, which provide a fertile site for rapid plant growth.

Easily the most abundant rooted plant infesting Spirit Lake is a species commonly called Eurasian milfoil. The significance of this well-known species is fourfold. First, milfoil is regarded as one of the most troublesome "nuisance weeds" in North American lakes and reservoirs, and is almost impossible to eradicate once it has become established. Second, milfoil is often associated with lakes that have undergone accelerated eutrophication (lake aging). Third, milfoil probably invaded Spirit Lake sometime after the 1980 eruption and now grows luxuriantly in shallower, more fertile post-eruption lakewaters. (There are no records showing that milfoil existed in Spirit Lake prior to the eruption.) And fourth, because access to Spirit Lake is still greatly restricted and is off-limits to recreation of any sort, milfoil was probably introduced to the lake by waterfowl flying in from milfoil-infested lakes and ponds located nearby.

Milfoil, like a malignancy, is both invasive and incurable. It will continue to grow and will likely suffocate the lake with its spreading abundance. Ironically, it was nature and not humankind that carried this pernicious plant to Spirit Lake. Ironically too, this bountiful life and not volcanic destruction will be the instrument of death and lake extinction.

CALLAHAN

Love and Boundaries

or How I Learned I could Push the Button

by Jerome Gold

For two weeks one summer a few years ago I participated in a war game. You've seen movies in which war games are played on boards, the players using tiny representations of airplanes and ships. The war game I took part in was similar to those. The difference lay in the fact that this was an Army game played on a board representing a portion of the European land mass, with no provision for naval support and minimal support from the Air Force. There were cardboard tabs, each about the size of the fingernail on your small finger, and these represented battalions, tank and infantry and artillery. Printed in black on each tab was a unit designation. Tabs denoting Russian units were colored red. Each tab represented 600 to 1,000 men.

The war was to begin in Germany but neither the Western European countries nor the Warsaw Pact countries, save the Soviet Union, had troops on the board. The battle would be fought Russians against Americans, Americans against Russians, at last.

While officers from some of the NATO countries observed the play and got acquainted with the players, the players themselves, on both sides of the board, were Americans. The American side was manned by officers with Anglo-Saxon surnames, the Russian side by officers with East European names. Whoever decided which man would play on which side had a sense of humor. Although my closest European ancestry is Russian, Polish and Lithuanian, I played on the American side. My name is westernized, and for purposes of the game this was apparently all that was required to identify me as a good guy, regardless of family history and migrations.

The game was played according to a computerized script, more or less. The "Russians" were more constrained by the script than the Americans, perhaps because we know less about the Russian army, and what we do know is abstract rather than subtle and personal, and so is more amenable to computerization. The game was scripted so that the Russians would attack across the East German border and eight days later would overrun American resistance in that part of eastern West Germany we — the Americans on the board — occupied.

In the late '70s the United States espoused the idea that yes, we reserve the right to nuke Russians but only after they nuke us. So it was on the board: both the Russians and the Americans had a nuclear capability but American policy prohibited first use. It was different with chemical and biological agents: although the Russians had these and could be expected to use them, they were not in our arsenal.

We were for the most part reservists and National Guardsmen. We had been brought to this southern military post for two weeks in lieu of summer camp. There were, I heard, more than 2,000 of us as well as several hundred active Army personnel, though only 100 of us were board players, all the others playing at staff assignments at the various levels of command, passing paper. Most of us arrived on the weekend, and, after settling in, we searched out others with whom we could establish a degree of agreeability. I had flown in from Seattle, and I found myself gravitating toward the far westerners, the Californians and Oregonians and Washingtonians. But I was also drawn to a coterie from the D.C. area. They were cops in civilian life, federal and municipal. A couple were of the bureaucratic variety, managers — these were the feds. The others were city cops and worked narcotics and could be very rough indeed.

I liked these cops, especially the narcotics cops, because they reminded me of men I had known when I was in the real Army in Vietnam. There was the kind of paranoia about them that I knew from that time and which is the single distinguishing feature between people whose lives are routinely at risk and people who, deep down, believe themselves safe. It is a functional kind of paranoia in that it serves to keep its victim alive. It is the opposite kind of disease from that which allows its victims to deny the immediacy of the threat.

The game began on Tuesday morning when the Russians attacked. All along the border between the two Germanies the Russians outnumbered us by a ratio of not less than six to one. In terms of artillery we were outnumbered thirteen to one. Where they attacked, our line indented, then bent, then held. This was as far as we got on Tuesday. There was some dead time, a glitch or two to be worked out of the computer, but everything was novel, we players were still introducing ourselves to one another, and we were enjoying it all. That evening I ran, had dinner in the mess hall, and read until I fell asleep.

On Wednesday we picked up where we'd left off. There was really no stopping the Russians, there were simply too many of them. We tried local counterattacks when we had the opportunity but these were only another way to lose men. We began our withdrawal.

After lunch one of the men with whom I'd flown out from Seattle brought a friend to meet me. They hadn't seen each other since they were together in Vietnam. The friend had another friend who had been at Pleiku around the time I was there.

We talked about how the fighting had been around Pleiku during that time, then about how it was in the parts of Vietnam each of us knew. It was old stuff now, we each had our platitudes ready, our codes by which two or three words signified paragraphs.

It was a nice interlude but when I was called to return to the board I was glad for the excuse to say goodbye.

That night several of us from Seattle plus the cops from D.C. and environs had dinner at a steak house in town. After dinner, talk over drinks. War talk again. People we knew. One of the guys I didn't know mentioned someone I had known, a master sergeant who, even before his death, had become a part of Special Forces' oral tradition. His team, the story-teller said, had been inserted into the North. The choppers had dumped them and taken off. Twenty minutes later the sergeant called for exfiltration. His team had been ambushed, they were on the run. Bring those choppers back.

A colonel who was also a legend in his own time was monitoring the operation from base. This man was legendary for his callousness. When he was told that the sergeant wanted to exfiltrate, his response was: "Fuck 'im. He hasn't been out long enough." The entire team was lost.

The story was hearsay, of course. But it struck a nerve. We had all known high-ranking people no less callous than our scapegoat. A doctor who refused to interrupt a night's drinking to tend a boy's shattered hip. An operations officer who refused to send a helicopter to evacuate a soldier in the throes of malarial convulsions. Having known such people in such circumstances not only made the story of the sergeant and the colonel who betrayed him plausible and comprehensible, but also confirmed our notion that the System, *our* System, was cruel and corrupt and was not deserving of sacrifice.

On Wednesday, following the day's board play, I, in the role of brigade intelligence officer, had established minefields where I believed the Russians were likely to move next. Now, on Thursday morning, on their first play they moved into the mined areas. We Americans had not used mines in the play before, and it threw the Russians. They demanded evidence that I had in fact laid mines the previous evening. I showed a referee the list of grid coordinates I had plotted to denote minefield boundaries. The referee was satisfied.

"Why didn't they go off when you crossed the minefield?" one of the Russians demanded. We had withdrawn across one of the mined areas but we had not set off the mines.

"They're command-detonated!" an engineer officer shouted at him, meaning that the mines were set off by somebody hiding in the bushes with a blasting machine, waiting for the precise moment to crank the handle, rather than set off by the pressure of tanks rolling over them.

The Russian snorted at the engineer's retort. He did, he actually snorted and put his nose in the air.

But the mines made little difference. The Russians were slowed for an hour or two, then regained their momentum. Our withdrawal was losing its sense of order; I saw the possibility of a route. There were just so unbelievably many Russians. We received intelligence from a superior headquarters that a second Russian army was closing on the heels of the one we faced, and that elements of the second echelon were wearing protective clothing. If true, this meant we could expect a chemical attack.

When play ended on Thursday we were in bad circumstances. The game was ceasing to be fun. I stayed late, plotting new minefields.

I woke up on Friday exhausted. The game resumed. What on Thursday we knew was going to happen to us actually began to happen. The Russians, having broken our line the previous day, were pressing hard, fragmenting us and isolating the fragments and then — insult of insults! — ignoring us as they continued their push west. At ten o'clock the game controllers stopped action. They told us we were free until one o'clock and should return to the game then.

At one o'clock we hung around waiting for the controllers to announce the resumption of play. Finally, at one-thirty, they told us to come back on Monday. They said the script had to be modified. It called for the Americans to be overrun eight days from the time the Russians crossed the border. Given the current situation, we would be overrun before the end of the day today if we continued play.

Over the weekend I was immensely tired and could not get enough sleep.

On Monday the Russians hit us with artillery-fired mustard gas. The gas attack was followed by a massive Russian assault that carried us through the end of the day and well into Tuesday. By Tuesday afternoon we were throwing battalion after battalion against the Russians and the Russians were swallowing them whole. None lasted more than a single move on the board, say, thirty minutes at most. Thirty minutes to lose a thousand men. Thirty minutes to lose a second thousand. We could have lost them faster if we had been reinforced faster. It became increasingly difficult to remember that these tabs representing battalions were, after all, only bits of cardboard. Finally it became impossible to regard them as anything but constructions first of living, then of dead, flesh. I was beginning to see individual faces.

One of my duties was to report intelligence — that is, information which might help planners work out an appropriate response to the Russian onslaught — to Division, our superior headquarters. My commander wanted me now to call Division and report the battle as though it were actually occurring. "Describe the tanks burning, the smell of the oil and the smoke, the bodies hanging out of the hatches, men screaming. Tell them what it's like."

I told myself that what my commander wanted of me had nothing to do with either the game or war — I am not an actor, I told myself — and I renewed my absorption in the progress of the game on the board. The matter of manufacturing battle casualties aside from those that were manufacturing themselves inside my head I let fall of its own weight.

There is the old saw about having to regard your enemy as less than human so that you can kill him. Perhaps that is true. But a corollary would be that you regard those of your own side as somehow superior not only to your enemy but to humanity at large; this, I suppose, because the sacrifices individual soldiers must make so that their squad or platoon may survive demand that the squad or platoon be worthy of this altruism.

My heart was breaking. A few battalions, here and there, clung to the slopes and the hilltops. They were all that was left of us. I did not feel hatred for the Russians. They were simply a force, as the rest of the world was a force, aligned to destroy the only people on earth I cared about. Out of love and blindness I could destroy the world. Had the war been for real, and had I nuclear weapons at my disposal, I was convinced that I would have used them. Even with the knowledge that I would be destroying the world, I would have done it.

The game left off for the day.

On Wednesday I was sick. My throat was sore. My ears hurt when I swallowed. I was feverish. At the board the American ranks were deflated by fully a third of the original players. Flu, severe colds. A couple of the Russians were ill too.

Play commenced, but it was stupid now. We were beaten. As fighting units our battalions no longer existed. Then something odd occurred: the Russians withdrew, conducting an orderly retrograde almost to where the play had begun at the border between the Germanies.

At the back of my mind flapped the flag of caution but my view of it was hindered by the elation I felt. Why were they withdrawing? Did they believe that we had beaten them? This happens in war: the victor takes such punishment that he imagines himself to have been beaten. If this was the case now, then we should counterattack. Or maybe there was peace and we had not yet been informed. Or maybe — and I knew this was laughable even as I thought it — the whole thing had been a mistake and the Russians, realizing this, were now trying to rectify the error.

We didn't counterattack immediately. We did not believe ourselves capable of mounting an assault. We had been whipped so thoroughly, we were paralyzed with the fear of what they would do to us if we joined them in combat again.

"You're defeating yourselves," our commander told us. "You're talking yourselves into a loser's mentality. You have to attack."

It was dumb. We had almost nothing left with which to attack. And then we attacked and were pushed back and we had less than almost nothing.

Then they nuked us.

It was what the flapping flag I'd glimpsed earlier was trying to warn me about. Probably some of us had expected it, those who were more detached, but I could not claim anything like detachment in this game and I could see by the faces of the Americans in the room that few of them could either.

Yet the nuking was anticlimactic. It was not more horrifying than what had already been done to us. We had learned fear, been taught to cower. Horror comes from self-knowledge and we had learned more about ourselves than it might be possible to forget. The nuking taught us nothing new.

But it did end the game. A single missile had landed in our rear, inflicting fifteen percent casualties (Hah! Right!) and cutting us off from supply and reinforcement. The Russians attacked again and we fought with what we had until the last battalion was surrounded, with no hope of breaking out. This took about ninety minutes.

Throughout the final hour and a half we waited for the American response, the counter-nuking. Approval had to come from above, time would be lost while committees met, allies were informed, et cetera. Still, I knew, we would return nuclear fire. This was the purpose of the game, wasn't it? To show us how it could happen that nuclear weaponry, its use, would be a necessity, how we could feel its necessity? Wasn't this why the game's designers had the Russians use nukes, even after they had beaten us? To justify our response?

But there was no response. The game was over. The controllers thanked us for our participation and turned us loose. No response: it occurred to me that perhaps what the Army had intended was to bring us to the point of making the decision to nuke and then to allow each of us to complete the gestalt for himself. But the notion of gestalt was too subtle for the Army; the Army had no faith in the individual's doing anything unless intimidated or coerced. No. I thought that what the Army intended by the game was to confront us with the possibility of nuclear warfare and to get us to accept that it might well occur. I wondered whether the Army's behavioral scientists knew that some people, in particular circumstances, might actually want to obliterate the world, and that love and loyalty could be the motivation.

I had dinner with the other Seattleites and the two guys with whom we'd dined the week before. We talked about how it would be to break into our lives again when we returned home. One of us had to fly down to Mexico immediately upon getting back to Seattle. He liked Mexico but he was spending most of every month there and he was tired of the travel. Another of us had recently left his wife and was living with a younger woman but that wasn't working out. He was thinking about trying to get onto active duty again. The past couple of weeks had been a vacation, we agreed, a getting away from routine.

Depressurization at descending into Sea-Tac the following evening compacted the mucus in my sinuses so that I thought my eardrums would burst. By the time we were on the ground I had given myself up completely to the pain in my head. I luxuriated in it, thinking of nothing at all.

TEA

by KURT CASWELL

I have begun to shout into the ears of poison ivy. It tells me there is nothing I say that it will find sense in. I tell it exercise disguise, put an alternate shape into your leaves, do not display yourself so slick like a candle,
show some restraint. It gasps at my suggestions and does not believe me
when I tell it of the comfort in drinking tea.

It is the leaves I want. To drink the tea of such a creature — a plant of
poison — would bring me strength, reinstall a sense of unconfined hope.
So I tempt poison ivy with water and fresh humus and the notion of going
incognito through the forest. I want its poison toned down, muted for the
cause of my first steeping. But it does not take any notice of the seriousness
in my request. It plays out its leaves, waxy and glossed as fresh as Varathane.

I have been four times now to this patch of poison ivy by this river. Each
time I go away, small, red blisters appear around my ankles where my socks
do not cover. And this, even after I have showered and washed with lye
soap.

Such a plant this is. I want its tea.

I believe the most vulnerable day for poison ivy is when the rain comes.
The first rain this season, I shall walk into the trees along the river to collect two leaves to steep my tea. I will not wear gloves. I will not wear shoes.
I will go naked into the ivy to show I am not afraid and mean to keep a
peace. The hair beneath my arms, between my legs, over my head and on
my limbs may give this plant a false pretense of concern. I will shave. Go
hairless like a two-hour-old mouse, and stand, bald and streamline like the
salmon, at the edge of the river to speak, softly this time, into the ears of
poison ivy and request two leaves. Two leaves is a very humble request.

They say it is common, occurs frequently now among men who are nei ther homosexual nor drug users, that it can be passed by women. Mine was contracted through blood transfusion. That is all I really know.

This is new to me. I understand nothing of it. There is no way for me to know what is to come. As if I have lost my legs and cannot walk, my eyes and cannot see. I am alone is this. I always have been.

"Poison ivy. POISON IVY. Give me your tea."

I have seen news files of patients. The lesions. The emaciation of the shoulders and how the face becomes a skin-covered skull. They do not speak well. They cannot stand. They are lucky to keep food down.

I am not showing symptoms, but have been diagnosed as positive for the virus. And next week they will test again for accuracy. I do not expect the results to change.

I am hairless. Storm vulnerable. I walk upright exposing my vitals — heart, lungs, genitals. I am moving swift now toward the river, the branches of rhododendron dragging long pock-lines through my skin. In places there is blood.

It is beginning to rain. I feel the heavy drops splash and scatter over my shiny skull. They trickle down into the corners of my eyes. Into my ears. Into my mouth. It is not a cold rain. The clouds are thick like wool and make the land feel warm. The drops bead and hang from the tips of the vine maple leaves — the secret acrobatics of water. The leaves bend, they grow closer to the ground as if they mean to fall from their posts. A wolf spider finds shelter beneath them — crawls there with black and red gran-ules of soil affixed to its footless appendages which are pointed and yet do not sink into the earth it treads so lightly. Maybe it is mere illusion, but the forest has a kind of vegetable language in the rain. You cannot hear it. But it is more easily distinguished than common speech along the street.

The stones at the river's edge are spotted with dark patches of rain. The water runs over their spherical forms and drips around the edges. My feet slip over these stones, sometimes painfully, sometimes easily. I leave no prints. I have no hair on my toes.

I can see the patch of poison ivy from where I stand — slick riparian village. It moves gently under the tone of the rain. It looks to be waving.

An otter emerges onto the flat rocks across the river. He is smooth like a seal. Black. And streamline. His nose is designed for breaking through the water. His limbs are disguised fins. He looks at me — tall and as slick as he — and disappears into the river.

I move to the edge of the river and enter up to the tops of my knees. The poison ivy is 100 yards downstream on my side of the bank. There is a sudden pain like ill-fit acupuncture, then cool relaxation. I am in the current and diving beneath the surface. My movement is fluid and unhurried. I am white like an ice barge through the water. My eyes are open. Something brushes my left calf and comes up along my ribs. The otter swims under and away from me. I surface, breathe, and dive again.

I judge 100 yards and raise myself up before the patch of poison ivy. I am cool and smell of salmon — greasy to the touch.

The poison ivy still waves beneath the dropping water from the sky. I walk among the leaves and stand motionless. There is an abrupt hush. It knows I am here. I kneel, bow my head, and prepare to speak.

"Poison ivy," I say in my muted voice. "Tone down, allow the waxy silk to run with the rain. Give me two leaves."

I take two leaves of poison ivy, fold them carefully and tuck them behind my left ear.

The wood is wet. I kindle a small fire on the floor of the atmosphere of the earth. I sit close, crisp, and shivering. The fire burns smoky. I lean into the cloud and breathe my lungs full of the deep fir taste.

I have laid the poison ivy out to dry. It is curling at the edges, becoming brittle, glass-like. I turn the leaves over every 14 minutes. I have trained myself to recognize this length of time.

The wood I gathered has tightened and burns clean. The fire comes up thin and red. The rain is light. I do not feel it across my bare skin for all the heat.

I walk out into the river to search for a flat stone. I find one with a bowl-like depression in its back, leave the water trapped there, and carry it into the fire. Flames splay out around it.

Already small red blisters are beginning to form near my ankles and up my shins. I go on with my work.

I am afraid to tell anyone. My wife. My parents. My sisters. I cannot know what to expect. I am not sure this is real. I have had more vivid dreams. But I know it is.

"POISON IVY. Poison ivy I will have your tea."

The stone is red. It glows and the water boils from the edges. I skim the surface with a fern leaf to lift the ashes of wood. The leaves of poison ivy are in my hand, dry and delicate as fall. I put three small jagged-edged stones into my palm, hold out my arm, and crush the leaves into the boiling water.

Blisters form suddenly on my hands. They itch. I look down at my naked legs. They are red and dotted with sores. I touch one. It is full of poison.

I remove the stone from the fire with my bare hands and stand back behind a fir tree, a downed log, move from position to position, keeping out of sight to watch the tea. Steam rises. The stone cools. The tea is steeping.

My palms itch. The stone has burned the blisters and they leak poison out onto my raw skin. I try to keep attention on the tea. But places along my legs itch, up my forearms to my elbows, under my chin. I know this is false, too early for the poison to work my skin. But the itching grows and I feel it over my bald skull.

The water in the stone is a deep purple. The poison ivy has gone to the bottom. The tea is ready.

The itching. I resist going back to the river to cool the rash, the burn. There are red blisters drawing out from my face. My back. The undersides of my feet. My eyes cloud. I cannot see well. My throat swells with red blisters. I feel the need for breath. I cannot get enough air.

Bending, I cup my hands beneath the bowl-shaped stone, lift, and drink.

The tea is bitter. It is like cayenne curling the edges of my tongue. My throat is thick and will not swallow. I have the impulse to heave the contents of my stomach, drain the tea from my mouth onto the ground. But I hold, and there is a softening. I swallow and the tea flows into the cavity of my chest, warm through to my knees and ankles. The light returns to my eyes. My hands are free of blisters.

I carry the empty stone back to the river, turn, and run white through the green forest.

Ladies in Differing States of Grace

by Susan Stanley

Sitting at my kitchen table, I mend a white batiste christening gown. Made over a half-century ago, it was presented by one of our father's parishioners for the baptism of my oldest sister in 1936. Somehow, it has fallen into my possession. (Who knows how these things happen? My own children, half-Jewish daughters of a lapsed Episcopalian mother, never wore it.)

Our British friends are taking two-month-old Marcus back to England for his christening. For a variety of good reasons, this is a miracle baby, a smiling charmer adored by a lot of people rippling beyond his family circle. His paternal grandfather, who died when this babe was a tadpole swimming in his silent sea, was, like my own father, an Anglican priest. It is fitting, I think, that this wonderful baby should wear our christening gown, and I find myself humming long-forgotten hymns as I sew.

A diligent search through the dross in the spare bedroom has turned it up, though without its featherstitched underslip. I see that a bit of lace has separated from the gatherings in the bodice, and from a ruffle along the hem. Examining it carefully, I realize for the first time that the entire gown is handsewn, down to the tiniest stitches in the French seams. The rows of tucks running the length of the front are all stitched by hand. Lace is set in stitch by tiny stitch. I've sewn since I was a very small girl, and continue to find great pleasure plying my needle. My mending stitches are adequate, but I'm no match for my father's parishioner, who surely went to her reward long ago. Even my thread looks like rope next to her exquisite handwork.

I sit in a chair beside my friend, who is dying. She is just a couple of years older than I, and I've had the honor of helping with her care. After months of being probed and prodded and pricked, x-rayed and scanned, tapped and taped and tormented, she lies now in this nursing home. She wears diapers, is fed by spoon, makes strange gurgling sounds, and doesn't seem to recognize people. A couple of months ago, I was telling her how much I had cherished our friendship over these many years. She reached out her right hand, the one that still worked, and touched my wet cheek, curious as a friendly baby. Sometimes, when I hold her hand, she smiles, though that happens less often as the days go by.

It doesn't matter to me that my words are probably a senseless gabble to her now. I speak to her anyway, of the things we once did together.

Remember the Fourth of July when I still lived in the big old red house, and we spent the day pruning the rose bushes back, and you were so fierce about it? And I railed at you, certain they'd never bloom again? And later that summer they bloomed better than they ever did before? Remember that afternoon? She makes the gurgling noise, and raises her eyebrows.

Heartened, I continue.

Remember the night I called you at two in the morning? Because I was so heartbroken about my whole wretched life: the divorce after so many years of marriage, my inability to find a job? And I was crying, and you drove over and gathered up what was left of me, and took me over to your place and put me into a flannel nightie and tucked me into the spare bed? Remember that? She flops her head to the other side, eyes unfocused, tired of the game.

I'm not.

Remember all the nights we used to go out to hear jazz, when we'd run into everybody we knew, and we'd stay 'til they closed? Remember how much fun that was?

And all those dinner parties I used to have? And we'd sit around and eat my soup and homemade bread and pour another glass of that godawful generic-label wine from Safeway, having a terrific time while we all loudly bemoaned the state of the world? Remember that?

Peaceful, she falls asleep for a few minutes, then awakens, sobbing with the cries of a little girl whose new doll has broken on Christmas morning. I try to comfort her, then go plead with the nurses to give her something. It takes a long time for the medication to take effect, and I hold her, stroking her hair, trying to think of songs to soothe her. All that come to mind are mournful Appalachian tunes.

"Black is the color of my true love's hair," I croon softly, "his face is somethin' wondrous fair...the clearest eyes and the strongest hands...I love the ground whereon he stands..."

Digging deeper into remembered Nebraska schooldays, I come up with others: "He's Gone Away," "I Gave My Love a Cherry." Another begins, "One morning bright and early, I saw a maid a' riding..."

After a half-hour or so, she sleeps. It's a heavy, drugged slumber, mouth open, sour breath expelled with each exhalation.

Keeping my friend company on her last, mysterious journey has been both wonderful and terrible. Gratifying, certainly. (How often, after all, are we given the opportunity to perform an act of pure love, no strings attached?) It is, I have come to believe, something akin to achieving a state of Grace. If I don't go see her every day or two, if only to watch her sleep, something is missing. While it's tiring, saddening, occupying a huge part of my heart, I find myself wondering at lives that leave no room for such tasks. Another dear friend of long standing remembers her father saying that 80 percent of life is simply in the *showing up*. I understand that now, in a way I didn't a year ago.

I've never spent time in a nursing home before, and this one, we decided, is very good, far and away the best we could find. It's filled with very old people, of course, and with the women who care for them: the youngish and middle-aged nurses, the cheerful and chattery young aides. The residents are mostly ancient women, their wispy white hair sometimes covered with those weird curly grey-brown wigs old ladies often wear. ("*Howard*," calls out one of them constantly, in a quavering, authoritative voice. "*Howard! Dorothy!*" She's calling them in from their summer play to wash up for dinner, I think.)

My friend is in a room with a woman who confided, one long rainy afternoon, that she is 91. She can scarcely see, this dear woman, but when I bring close to her eyes the small crib-sized quilt I've been working on these recent weeks, she speaks longingly of the needlework she once did.

Always — always! — there are fresh roses and other flowers, home-grown and home-arranged by the old woman's children and grandchildren. They fill the room with their extravagant fragrance, mingling with the nursing home smells of medicines and human bodily wastes.

Sometimes, the nurses tell me, they come into the room to find the nearly-blind 91-year-old woman has wheeled herself over to the other bed, and is holding my friend's hand, stroking it and talking softly to her, speaking words they cannot hear.

In the Country Above

by Nancy Lord

A Dena'ina Indian story tells of a man who fell in love with a woman he found in the woods chewing spruce gum. He took her home and they lived together, but she ate only brush and sometimes she disappeared and came home soaking wet. One time he followed her and found her swimming with beavers. She was a beaver-woman. She took him into her beaver house, taught him to swim and to eat tender branches. When fall came she told him he could go, but he didn't want to. She changed him into a beaver and they lived at the lake all the time after that. Now and then they changed into people, but mostly they were perfectly happy to remain beavers.

I don't know if this story is meant to be instructive or cautionary, or simply an entertainment, but I think about it as I walk to the lake above the cabin where we spend summers. Here, some distance down the out-flow creek from the lake, beaver have built two new ponds that have flooded the trail and opened the forest.

I stand below the first dam and touch a piece of it, a butt end of alder, faceted with the cuts of chisel-wide teeth. I wonder: how is it possible that mud and *sticks*, none of them larger around than my wrist, can be holding back that eye-level expanse of flat, sun-glistened water? As I watch, fish surface with a sound like soap bubbles bursting, leave tiny ringed ripples. They're no more than fingerlength, rainbows that might have washed over the older dam at the end of the lake. Across the pond, a bush shakes; a bird I can't see is working through it, picking buds. Bird song is everywhere — the wistful, burry tones of the thrush, the trilling of warblers. Water trickles through the dam. A breeze rustles past, turning alder leaves to show their paler sides. With a crack of wings, two ducks take off from the far end of the pond; pintails, they whistle across a cloudless sky.

Only two years ago this was a shady forest of dark, moss-hung spruce and twisted birch, head-high thickets of devil's club, mossy humps of mouldering logs. Passing through on the trail we could just hear the gurgle of creek, buried somewhere within. But the beavers have altered the landscape. There are more in this country now than we've ever seen, and they've moved outward from the lake, felling enormous trees, engineering waterways. Each spring, we see ousted young ones down on the inlet, paddling through salt water in search of new territories.

I look across the pond to a sunny slope of meadow, a purple patch I know to be new violets. After a winter of heavy snows and periodic volcanic dustings, spring has come to this part of Alaska, finally taking the past patches of gray snow from the woods. Late May, and the ferns are just unfurling, the devil's club leafing on its cudgel end. It's possible now as it never is later in the year to move through the country, to see its beginnings, its contours, and its history.

Ken calls from up ahead. Always the pragmatist, he's checking out the blueberry bushes, examining buds, predicting a good harvest. He wants to know if I remember when our first pie was, last year. It was when we were still fishing hard, still in July. I remember because I hadn't wanted to take the time to pick berries, but later I was glad we had.

I continue along the trail, thinking again of the Dena'ina. They hunted beaver, roasted their tails on sticks, used their fur for hats and sleeping robes. They lived with beaver, shared the country with them, respected them. The story suggests the Dena'ina believed a beaver's life was as legitimate as any other. It was not a ridiculous idea, in their world, to imagine a human choosing a beaver's life.

But the Dena'ina who used to be here are gone. After European, Russian, and American contact, their descendants lived in villages along the coast, where they adopted the Russian Orthodox religion and lived by fishing and working in canneries. A village site just a few miles from here wasn't abandoned until the late 1920s, when its remaining inhabitants moved north to join another village and send their children to school. Other Dena'ina, today, have disappeared into the prevailing culture.

Uphill through a tunnel of alder, we straddle the center of the muddy path, the tracks of a moose. We whoop at the top, giving notice to any bear on the other side. There it is, through the birch leaves: the lake.

We call it "the lake" or "the lake above our camp." On maps, among thousands more Alaskan lakes, it hasn't any name. Locally, we've heard two names: Horseshoe Lake, after its shape, and Hayden Lake, after our neighbor, who lives a couple of miles distant and who, when we asked him the lake's name, gave it his own.

I'm very fond of our neighbor and, after fifty summers here, he's earned his connections to this country. Still, naming pieces of the landscape after ourselves, after *people*, doesn't seem right. We leave enough mark on the country as it is.

The Dena'ina didn't name places after people. Neither did individuals, as far back in history as anyone knows, ever coin new names; the names were already there, reaching back through generations of oral tradition. When Dena'ina place names were collected from those who still speak the language, remarkable consistency was found among the speakers. Names were reported with care and with obvious affection for associations with them. A hill is known as Where an Animal is Crouching because, from a certain vantage, it looks like a large animal preparing to spring. A hunting area is called Where Horns Are Gathered. A river is called Where Someone Put a Man's Head Under Water, commemorating a time, a story, when two men fought over a fish.

A mountain ridge we can see from our camp is known as Ridge Where We Cry. Shem Pete, one of the oldest living Dena'inas, reported in 1982, "They would sit down there. Everything is in view. They can see their whole country. Everything is just right under them. They think about their brothers and their fathers and mothers. They remember that, and they just sit down there and cry. That's the place we cry all the time, 'cause everything just show up plain."

The Dena'ina knew some of their lakes as Lake of Creek that Flows Swiftly, Grass is There Lake, Overturned Trees Lake, Water Lily Lake, Lake in Which There Are Beaver Lodges. The lake above our camp would have had a name. We can only imagine what it might have been.

We cross the lake by creaking rowboat, escaping mosquitoes — the first of the season, the oversized, sluggish ones that wintered inside niches of tree bark. Ken rows; I sit in the stern, stare into the black water, the sun hot on my head. *Plok.* I turn to see widening rings near the shore.

I look back at the dead, broken tree that always looks to me, especially in evening light, like an antlered moose. In that low spot past it, twice, I've seen moose sunk to their knees, browsing. A week before, a bear was grubbing through the same area. Ken saw it here; I saw it later, looking over the bluff at our camp, a large blond bear with a dark stripe down its back.

There's beaver sign everywhere. Fresh, yellow cuttings. Flattened trails emerging from the brush, ending in water. The first house is partway down the lake, sprouting green alders from its roof. We creak past. I watch for a reddish beaver we've often seen here — the same one, or different ones from year to year, I don't know — but none appears. Another fish jumps. This is a good fishing spot; the rainbows like to shelter amid the underwater branches.

Ken stops rowing, fills a plastic bag with lake water, drinks from the corner of it as it spurts from pin holes in its side. I say what I say every time we come to the lake: "This is my favorite place in the world."

The lake narrows, turns. Lily pads cross the narrows. Dead, gray, weathered-to-a-shine tree trunks stand in water at the edges, a sign that the lake has risen over the years. Around the curve, down the lake's other leg, we would come to the outlet, the beaver dam, the best of the blueberry bushes. We spot a single loon on that side; it dives and comes up again. Another beaver house rises like a haystack against a stretch of grass-covered flat. The mountains lie that way, the high passes the Dena'ina crossed to first come to this country, sometime between three hundred and a thousand years ago. Today, the mountains are lost in billowy clouds.

We land the boat on a point.

We hike away from the lake, into sun-dappled forest. We kick up clouds of ash, circle hollows of devil's club, climb over downed trees. Salmonberry are already in bloom, pink petals wide and silk-smooth. Here and there, last summer's highbush cranberries are still hanging on, reduced to wrinkled red shells. The Dena'ina used all of these plants. They ate the berries, but they also boiled the highbush cranberry bark as a cure for upset stomachs and colds. They ate the shoots, flowers, and berries of the salmonberry and made a tea from its leaves. This time of year, they ate the leaf clusters of the devil's club; they spit chewed stalk onto wounds as a painkiller, wrapped fractures in bark, and harvested the root to treat toothache.

The pit, when we come to it, is obvious. It's deep, a depression in the ground, perhaps four feet lower than the forest floor. It's not the depth that's so remarkable, but the exact rectangular shape, the outline of two rooms. One is perhaps fifteen by twenty feet, the other a third that size. Rimmed with ridges of earth, they're joined with a break in the wall between them. Another break opens the large room to the outside.

I've been here once before, but I'm still taken by surprise, still overcome by something I can't easily explain. I want to hold my breath, stop time, go back. People lived here. The country remembers. The land holds this memory in ridges of earth, in deep holes, in the cry of a jay and the smell of softened spruce pitch. The people of this country lived here. I don't want to move. I only want to be frozen in their presence, the marks they made, the lines they drew.

It was a long time ago, and it wasn't. It was before Captain Cook sailed by in 1778, before epidemics of smallpox, measles, whooping cough, flu, and tuberculosis wiped out entire villages. It was not so long ago that the land's forgotten. A wall. A doorway. How many feet walked through? How many stories were told?

A spruce tree — one of the largest in the area — grows from one corner of the main room; another, somewhat smaller, stands in the pit itself. Either must be at least a couple of hundred years old.

We call them house pits. They're common in this part of Alaska, wherever the hunting was good and there was water to drink and a reasonable winter climate. They're what's left of the traditional Dena'ina houses — barabaras, as they were called by the Russians. Winter homes. I try to picture this one as it had been — dug into the ground but then framed with short walls of posts and logs, surrounded with sod, a roof of overlapping sheets of birchbark or perhaps caribou hides, back when this was caribou instead of moose country. I try to see the barabara in snow, smoke curling from the hole in the roof, snowshoe trails beaten around it. A cache built off the ground, on peeled poles, filled with bales of dried salmon. The smell of boiling meat. Sounds of people talking, babies. Winter was a time of rest. January is known, in Dena'ina, as the Month We Sing.

Right now, King Salmon Month, the barabara would be silent, empty, the country's new grass closing in around it. The people would be on the beach below, camped in less substantial houses, feasting on fresh salmon, splitting and hanging salmon to dry in the smoke of an alder fire, beginning again the cycle of preservation that would see them through another winter.

Summers on the beach, we catch salmon to sell to Japan. We eat a few, hang some in our smokehouse. In The Month Leaves Turn Yellow, we leave the beach, not to this country above, but to a country away, a house in a city.

Archeologists have excavated a very few house pits, but they never found much in the way of artifacts of historical record. "Excessively tidy," one archeologist said of the Dena'ina. Unlike the Eskimo, who inhabited much of the same area at an earlier period and who left a wealth of stone, bone, and clay artifacts behind, the Dena'ina had a wood-based culture. They did without stone lamps, burning instead the tails of candlefish, an oily fish. Their containers were made from spruce root, birch bark, hollowed out logs. They walked about on wooden snowshoes, hunted beaver with clubs, furnished their homes with grass mats. They burned their dead. If I were to dig into this pit, I would most likely find only fire-cracked rocks from the hearth or from cooking — from being dropped, hot, into bark bowls filled with water.

We leave the pit, walk silently, farther into the woods. Everywhere, I think I see unnatural depressions, two walls forming a right angle; I know pits are here and I can't see them exactly, or what I see are only dead trees fallen and rotted, covered with moss. I know there must be more than one house to the village. We pick our way through brush, over more deadfall. We step to the rim of another pit: deeper than the first, smaller, two rectangular rooms of different sizes connected with a pass in the wall between, unmistakable.

The woods open to more sun, another lake without a mapped name, more beaver houses. An old cabin still stands on the hillside, just up from the shore. Half the roof has fallen in; across the other half lies a wooden sled, bleached white as bone. The front door opens inward to a mess of abandoned debris: torn fiberglass insulation, rotting clothes, an old boot, broken glass, rusted cans, a bare bed frame, swollen paperback books, and overturned washing machine. A television set, sitting upright on the floor, is entirely whole, in need only of a dusting.

I've been here before, though not for years. Moose antlers that were mounted over the door have fallen to the ground. Before, I pondered the meaning of a set of bird wings — white ptarmigan wings — nailed beside the door; all that remains now are the rusting nails with a bit of fiber caught beneath them. I look for a spruce root sewing basket I remember, its side rotted out where it lay against the floor, spilling buttons, but I can't find it.

Ken examines the woodpile, cords of rotten spruce. He finds the old well, bends aside an alder to free the hatch and look inside at the cribbing, the cool, clear water deep down.

All I know about the people who lived here I know from our neighbor, Hayden, who recalls delivering them once to the Anchorage airport, their cardboard suitcase tied together with the starter cord from an outboard. He remembers them, walking through the airport door, nervous and so out of place, "holding hands like two little kids."

Doris was Dena'ina, from the village to the north. Chet was white. Summers, they fished down on the beach. They were here in 1958; I know this because one of them pounded empty twenty-two shells into the end of a cabin log, spelling out their initials and that year. Hayden remembers when they bought their generator, television, washing machine. It was Doris's "Indian money," the one-time payment each member of her village received for oil exploration on their land. He also recalls that Chet got more and more "Indian" until he forgot how to write his name and could only sign papers with an X.

Out behind the cabin, under a big spruce, there's a dog's house of bent alders, branches, and grass. A rusted chain circles the tree, buried in the wood where the tree's grown around it, thick as scar tissue. Nailed to the tree, high, are two bear paws; most of the fur is gone now, exposing bone knuckles, and lichens have begun to cover the bone like new fur. I only know that the Dena'ina used dogs for hunting bear and that they tied bear paws around a dog's neck as part of its training.

Five years ago, the last time I was here, I pulled on the dog's chain. I was interested in how much new earth had built up around the tree. I pulled and dug and slowly tore the chain from the ground, and at the end I found, not only the end of the chain, but the dog's very skull.

The surface of the lake, down past the cabin, is creased. A small brown head: the apex of an expanding wake that flows behind, widening, widening and softening, merging at last into smooth water. I suspect there are more beaver here now than at any time since before the Dena'ina came through the mountains.

Ken and I sit on the slope above the lake and eat our lunch of brownies and apples. He's eager to leave; we have work on the beach, nets to finish hanging and a log to float on the high tide. He looks at his watch. It feels odd to both of us, to be where we can't see the ocean, to not have the tide as our timekeeper. I wish we didn't have to go. Who, today, dreams of living with beavers? For all the natural beauty here — the lake reflecting spruce and mountains, the bunchberry flowers growing beside me, the *sweet-sweet-*

sweet of a sparrow — I feel the loss, the absence, the missing continuum.

Those of us who come here only as visitors will never know what it was to live here, to be a part of this place. If I ever learn why people attached ptarmigan wings beside a door, I will still never, really, understand the meaning of that act. We can never know the feeling of looking down from a known place and wanting to cry — not at how beautiful the wild country is, but for our brothers and fathers and mothers, our history and our place where "everything show up plain."

Ken and I love this place, but we are starting with it almost from scratch, and without knowing what it is to live in it entirely, eating its animals and plants, making our lives out of wood. It is all we can do to begin our own year-to-year traditions, our own stories. We name our places: The Lake Above Our Camp, Where the Striped Bear Was, The Beaver House Where There Are Trout, Where the Berries Are Biggest. Down on the beach, we bought a fishing site from our neighbor, Hayden; he called it Eagle Set, after a tree where eagles liked to perch; the tree fell down and disappeared and the eagles roosted elsewhere, and still we call that location Eagle Set. The stories we tell are of people at airports, old cabins, a chain and a skull, ptarmigan wings beside a door and then no ptarmigan wings — nothing left but a spot of fiber between a nail and a rotting log.

The beaver, still swimming, looks like he's doing it for fun. I can only imagine that he may be trying to tempt us to join him.

When Brazilians brought
the Amazon Indians down
to the boomtown carved
from a forest once wet
with waterdrops plipping
the cool cupped fronds,
raucous as birds crying
at the sight of monkeys
fleeing from yellow eyes
stalking the night, they
took them packed aboard
a bus, bright with paint
fresh from native plants,
bold in their plumage,
fierce with their spears,
to see the city's shiny
new museum wing display
where Amazon Indian life,
reproduced down to sticks
and feathers, shed light
on a future closing fast.
The Indians smiled while
the interpreter grasped
for straws; on the ride
back to their shadowland,
they shook their heads
at how Brazilians survive
with no stands of trees
for cover, and screams
of beasts about to die
wheeling in their brains,
the bad air and hot sun.
It was good to be home.

by David Hedges

Indian Reservations

101

Delgam Uukw versus The Queen

by Terry Glavin

The trial — known formally as *Delgam Uukw versus The Queen*, Delgam Uukw being the first of the 54 chiefs named as plaintiffs in the action — had actually begun on the morning of May 11 in the Bulkley Valley town of Smithers. Back then the lawyers were talking about six months of trial time, but a few weeks into the trial it became evident that this was not going to be quite like any other trial in the history of challenges before the courts within the realm of Indian grievances commonly known as "land claims." Over the protests of the hereditary chiefs, the trial had been moved to Vancouver. It would be almost three years before all the evidence was in, the various parties would spend in excess of $20 million on research and legal fees, and even then it would not be over.

It didn't take B.C. Supreme Court Judge Allan McEachern long to realize that this trial was going to be very different from any he had dealt with during his 36 years as a lawyer and a judge. A hard-working, quick-witted, 61-year-old asthmatic, McEachern was also an eastside Vancouver boy, a brutal rugby player, a non-drinking, non-smoking Coca-Cola addict with little patience for anything that hinted of a court-room spectacle or a theatrical display. But before him was a case that demanded an unprecedented departure from normal rules of evidence, one that presented him with an uncomfortable range of rulings. At one extreme, he could hand down a decision that could in the end dismantle most of the Province of British Columbia and return it to the Indians. On another extreme, he could destroy more than a century of hopes held by the native people of Canada's Pacific slopes and perhaps

From *A Death Feast In Dimlahamid* by Terry Glavin, published by New Star Books, 2504 York Ave., Vancouver B.C. V6K 1E3, 1990.

change the course of history in a direction in which the indigenous peoples of Canada's far west would be left a mere shadow of a distant past.

Certainly there had been aboriginal rights cases before, throughout North and South America and throughout Britain's former colonies the world over, and McEachern had a well-travelled path of case law to follow. Various courts and legislatures had reluctantly grappled with the legal rights held by Indians ever since Charles V, the King of Spain, convened a junta of lawyers and theologians in 1550 at Valladolid in an effort to square conquest with justice in Spain's new "possessions" in Mexico and Peru. At Valladolid, the two leading antagonists were Juan Gines de Sepulveda, who held that some races were simply superior to others and some were destined to servitude, and Bartoleme de Las Casas, who argued that indigenous peoples of the newly discovered continent possessed inherent rights to sovereignty and freedom. Just how the participants concluded the debate is lost to history, and King Charles V entered a monastery soon afterwards. But in more than four centuries since Valladolid, Canadian law had still not quite settled either on the side of Sepulveda or in favour of Las Casas.

Throughout the 1970s and 1980s, in a growing number of cases before Canadian courts, judges were finding something that came as quite a surprise to most British Columbians: there was merit, after all, in the old Indian argument that Indian title to the land west of the Rockies — the greatest amount of which was "Crown" or public land — had not been clearly ceded to the Crown from the indigenous peoples who lived there. This might be Canada, but whether or not it was legitimately British Columbia was becoming increasingly unclear. Judges did not quite know where to turn, and neither did the forest companies, who were meeting stiff resistance from Indians as their loggers moved deeper into the hinterland with rapid-rate clearcutting technology and improved road networks. Neither did the fishing companies, who were finding their century-old monopoly on commercial fishing challenged in the courts by Indian fishermen who defied them to produce evidence that any Indians had ever surrendered rights to the coastal fisheries resources. Mining companies were roadblocked until they talked terms on Indian hiring quotas. Even the all-powerful railway companies were spur-lined with court injunctions by small groups of Indians who fished salmon with dipnets from precarious perches in the Fraser canyon.

Given the depth and breadth of the case before McEachern, the courts would have to come to that fork in the legal trail, to that place that already existed in the real world, and there would have to be some kind of decision, even though whatever McEachern decided could be challenged eventually by one interest or another to the Supreme Court of Canada, even to the United Nations, as had occurred in 1981 in the Lovelace case. That was the case in which Ottawa was backed into a corner by a UN human rights tribunal and forced to repeal a section of the Indian Act even though it had been upheld by the Supreme Court of Canada. The Act had denied Indian status to Indian women who married non-Indians, and it also denied status to their children.

The Gitksan and Wet'suwet'en were leading the indigenous nations on the Pacific slopes on this most crucial issue, the "land question." What the hereditary chiefs were seeking was a clear declaration from the courts that all their traditional lands were still unceded, that provincial law held no sway, that Gitksan and Wet'suwet'en house chiefs were the only legitimate authority in their territories. Before Canadians was the very real possibility that Dimlahamid was not a myth, that it was British Columbia that was the myth. It was a difficult notion for most British Columbians to comprehend. The uncertainty caused a state of affairs that demanded the attention of Canadian law.

It was becoming clear to most tribal leaders in British Columbia that even if they did get justice on the land question in the courts, there might be little left of the land's natural wealth when that day came. There seemed little sense in waiting for Ottawa's comprehensive claims process to unfold, or for a victory in *Delgam Uukw versus The Queen*.

In Gitksan and Wet'suwet'en country, where the logging industry provided the greatest cash income for the minority of employable Indian adults with full-time jobs, it was a challenge, a challenge Mas Gak described this way: "The roadblock is a test. You have husband against wife, brother against brother, and father against son, the whole thing with Indian-white relations, and all that plays itself out. But it's the kind of discussion we have to have."

And if the roadblock was indeed a test of the authority the chiefs claimed in *Delgam Uukw versus The Queen*, the Gitksans were clearly up to it. They had their own history of resistance to draw lessons from, all the way from the blockade of the Skeena River after the burning of Gitsegukla in 1872, through the battles with fisheries officers over the right to inland fisheries and the railway blockades at Gitwangak in 1985, and as the 1980s drew to a close, they could also look to the roadblocks erected by the Lubicons of

Alberta, the Innu of Labrador, the McLeod Lake Sekanis, the Tahltans of Telegraph Creek, and the Haidas of the Queen Charlotte Islands.

In some tribal territories, the law had been successfully used to put logging on hold while the question of aboriginal title remained unanswered. It was successfully used by the Nuu-Chah-Nulths at Meares Island in 1985, when the B.C. Appeals Court, the highest court in the province, granted an injunction against logging that spectacular little island off the west coast of Vancouver Island at the mouth of Tofino Harbour. The prevailing judgment, against the corporate giant MacMillan Bloedel, held that the Indians had for generations pressed the question of title, but "they have not been dealt with at all. Meanwhile, the logger continues his steady march and the Indians see themselves retreating into a smaller and smaller area. They, too, have drawn the line at Meares Island. The island has become a symbol to their claim to rights to the land." And the law was successfully used the following year at Deer Island, a small island between the mainland coast and Vancouver Island, in Kwagewlth territory. In that case, the Kwagewlths were able to use a "Douglas Treaty," one of that handful of colonial treaties on southern Vancouver Island, to prevail against Halcan Log Services in the Kwagewlths' campaign to maintain access to berry grounds, hunting areas, and gravesites. On the Queen Charlotte Islands, the inequity of B.C.'s traditional position in the courts was used to secure the Haidas' control of the entire southern portion of their island homelands, but only after 72 Haidas were arrested at a Lyell Island logging road blockade. The federal and provincial governments tried to find an easy way out by compensating the forest companies and declaring the south Moresby region a park reserve, but the Haidas knew it for the victory it was — a restoration of their sovereignty in the area. At McLeod Lake, a Sekani village deep in B.C.'s northern bush and within the arctic drainage area covered by Treaty Eight, Chief Harry Chingee had grown tired from years of waiting for recognition of his band's treaty rights. He set up a logging road blockade in defiance of a B.C. Supreme Court injunction, and in December 1988, he won from the courts an injunction preventing logging companies from clearcutting a vast area the Sekanis claimed as their treaty entitlement.

A formal attempt by the Gitksan and Wet'suwet'en to restrain unwanted resource extraction in their tribal territories had failed in 1987, when the B.C. Supreme Court refused their request for an injunction against new logging areas or Crown land pre-emptions while *Delgam Uukw versus The Queen* remained before the courts.

In the Gitksan and Wet'suwet'en territories, there were already 39 sawmills in operation by 1920. But they were small-scale outfits, and the forest industry developed slowly, at a pace the forests could sustain. Right up to the 1960s selective logging was practiced — only the best trees were cut, and traditional resource uses were not severely impacted. But with the advent of massive forest-clearcutting techniques, more lethal technologies and more productive mills with fewer workers, the scene was changing drastically particularly following the recession of the late 1970s. Westar Timber, the major company in the region with a whole log chipper and two sawmills all within an hour's drive from the fabled lost city of Dimlahamid, employed 600 workers by 1989, consuming 1.5 million cubic metres of wood a year, almost ten times as much as it had consumed ten years earlier. At the Gitksans' northwestern frontiers, another million cubic metres of wood that had been virgin forest in the 1970s was being cut and shipped in whole logs every year out of the region, and in some cases, straight out of the country to Asia.

By the time the tribal leaders' attempts at an interim land freeze had failed before the courts in 1987, two thirds of the chiefs' traditional territories remained virgin forest. But where there was logging, independent foresters working for Silva Ecosystems Consultants Ltd. found the countryside turning to moonscape. An 82-page report cited wholesale overcutting and mile-wide clearcuts. Merchantable timber was left on the ground to rot in "high-grading" operations — cutting all the trees and taking only the best — and the soil in some house chiefs' territories was reverting to its condition at the close of the last ice age.

Throughout the Gitksan-Wet'suwet'en territories, while *Delgan Uukw versus The Queen* proceeded slowly in B.C. Supreme Court, roadblocks were starting to turn up everywhere.

On February 11, 1988, at Little Oliver Creek, on the western frontier of Gitksan territory a few miles east of Terrace, the Gitksan frog clan chiefs of Gitwangak issued a notice to Skeena Cellulose and Tide Lake Logging that frog clan chief Luulak, Sandra Williams, would not permit any more logging on her house territory. Merchantable timber had been left to waste on the ground and some trees had been cut several yards from their base in what was obviously high-grading of good timber. About twenty Indians showed up at the site at 8:30 that February morning, warning the contractors to leave the area and informing them they had 24 hours to remove their equipment and if they did not heed the warning they would be treated as thieves. The RCMP was called in, but the three crew trucks backed off. "I don't want to have anything to do with this," Tide Lake's Frank Cutler said. "The Indians say they were never defeated and we never took their land. I don't know. I wasn't there." It was a clear and immediate victory. The next day, the police arrested Giila'wa, the 52-year-old eagle clan chief Peter Turley, on a charge of possession of stolen property. On Luulak's instructions, Giila'wa had removed a front-end loader that was left behind at the site. An angry Mas Gak said the case would be fought as far as needs be, pointing out that Giila'wa would be entitled to a trial by a jury of his peers — other Gitksan nobility — and further pointing out that Indians were effectively barred from jury duty in Canada until 1974, when jury selection was amended to permit selection from on-reserve voters lists. The case against Giila'wa was dropped.

Later that month, at about 3:30 a.m. on Monday the 29th of February, Mary Johnson, the 78-year-old Kispiox matriarch Antiigililbix, wrapped a traditional button blanket around her frail shoulders, walked through her old village, so famous for its totem poles, and stood at a bonfire in the middle of a logging road that dissects the reserve. Robert Jackson got into his pickup truck and with the help of a few of the younger men hauled a huge cedar log across the road, where on a normal day a fully loaded logging truck would pass every ten minutes in an annual convoy that took 500,000 cubic metres of wood, enough to build a city of 10,000 houses, out of the Kispiox Valley highlands. About twenty of the young men of the village were there already, and they stood around the blazing fire, stamped their feet on the frozen ground and tucked their cold hands deep into their pockets. Wii Seeks stood with them, beside Kispiox wolf clan chief Wii Muugalsxw, whose house territory entrusted to him under the Gitksan law of ascendancy was now in ruins, a barren ground several miles up the Kispiox Valley, scattered with cavernous pyramids of felled and discarded spruce trees. Wii Muugalsxw, who is the soft-spoken, 40-year-old Kispiox artist and carver Art Wilson, smiled nervously as the first logging truck showed up. Then the second, then the third, then the fourth, and it was all over the truckers' citizens band radio in minutes. RCMP Sgt. Fred Simpson arrived in his cruiser from Hazelton.

This wasn't Little Oliver Creek. This was one of the major conduits for timber supply in the entire northwest country. This time, things were going to be different, and Sgt. Simpson radioed in for backup.

Just before dawn, things turned nasty. There was confusion and shouting at first, and then trucker Jim Pierson turned and walked back to his truck. "This is bullshit," he said. "They've got enough already and yet they still have to screw us around." The other truckers followed Pierson, and by about 6 a.m. the truckers had set up their own roadblock on the far side of the Kispiox River bridge, within shouting distance of the village. If they couldn't get in, they weren't going to let the Indians out. Sgt. Simpson waited for word from the RCMP substation in Terrace, but there was still nothing definite. He talked the truckers into going home and waiting.

Then the sun came up. It was quiet around the fire, and the older women in the village brought tubs full of salmon chowder to the roadblock crew. Mary Johnson, old Antiigililbix, turned to the circle around the fire, and the men were quiet, and she sang them a song in the old language. And then she said, "I won't live much longer. I am standing here on behalf of myself, and my family, and my grandchildren and my great-grandchildren. They will be the ones to suffer all the trials and all the troubles." And then she sang some more.

Nothing moved, and the RCMP watched, wondering what to do. A few hours into the standoff, Sgenna, Delbert Turner, had agreed to move Robert Jackson's great cedar log to allow logging contractor Dave Webster to get his truck out from behind the barricade — Webster was among several truck loggers who were trapped inside the closed-off area when the blockade went up — on the understanding that Webster and the others would come to meet with the chiefs. But none of the truckers showed up at the Kispiox hall that night. More than 60 truckers had been turned away from their rounds through the Kispiox Valley, so after three hours of debate, the chiefs decided to leave Robert Jackson's cedar log where it had been hauled away from the road. Never mind putting it back on the road just yet, said Sgenna, thinking a little further down the road. There was an old-time feast, and the decision was to fight another day.

The following morning, a chartered bus carrying 30 RCMP officers in riot gear turned off Highway 16 into the parking lot of the Totem Café in the truckstop town of New Hazelton, a few miles from Kispiox. A second, empty bus rolling behind the first, in case it was needed to transport Indians arrested at the roadblock. The RCMP force had been assembled from Mounties in Prince Rupert, Terrace, and Smithers, and RCMP Supt. Ron Pettitt said it was a necessary "show of force" to see the blockade cleared. But the roadblock was already down.

Things were quiet again, for about two months.

On the morning of Thursday, May 5, on a road Westar Timber was pushing into rich forest lands on the northern frontiers of the Gitksan territories, Norman Larson of Al Larson Logging and six of his crewmen were on their way in to the head of the newly cleared road in the Salmon River area when they were stopped by seven Gitksans. There was no roadblock, just seven Indians who warned Larson's crew that they were trespassing on the house territory of Chief Gwoimt and would not be permitted to proceed further, and that they had until Saturday morning to get their equipment out of the area. Westar, the principal firm involved in the roadbuilding, had been invited months earlier to discuss its plans with the chiefs, but all the chiefs got were instructions to remove the traps from their traplines in the region.

The road was being built to provide a conduit for the timber Westar's mills needed in the Salmon River country, but its main function would be to provide a land connection to the vast forests north of the Babine River, in the territory of the old Gitksan villages of Kisgegas and Anlagasimdeex, a territory known to provincial forest ministry cartographers as the Sustut Block but known to the Gitksans as the house territories of their own chiefs, among them Wii Gaak (Neil Sterritt Sr.), Gitluudahl (Pete Muldoe), Wii Seeks (Ralph Michell), and Waigyet (Elsie Morrison, Ralph's grandmother). Standing with them as their neighbours were Miluulak, Tsabux, Wiiminosik, Luus, and Wiieelast. They were all fireweeds, frogs, and wolves. Eight forest companies were in competitive bidding for a licence to log 400,000 cubic metres of Sustut timber every year for twenty years, but Westar was clearly the front-runner, with the rest of the companies on the far side of the region, in the Prince George area. The Gitksans said they needed the area, too, and so did the caribou and grizzly bear populations, which would be decimated by clearcutting. It was a spectacularly rich and roadless expanse of wilderness, several hundred square miles of untouched forests and mountains with the highest concentrations of mountain goats west of the Rockies.

This was going to be it. It was one thing to highgrade the house territory of a chief west of Gitwangak. It was one thing to continue a regime of logging in the Kispiox Valley, where the provincial government had already committed the timber. But the chiefs had reached a decision on the government's plans to open up the northern territories with logging mains and sideroads: there would be no bridge across the Babine River.

For the other side, it was also time for a showdown. Keith Spencer, Westar's new manager of the company's northwest operations, said it was simply a police problem, and he would expect the police to act. There was no way the company could back off when a third of its anticipated timber supply in the coming years was at stake. As for all this carry-on about Gitksan house territories and unsurrendered Indian land, Spencer, only a few weeks on the job, said: "It's rubbish." Sgt. Simpson was called in again. He headed up the Salmon River road, said hello to everyone, and decided to "monitor" the situation this time, "in a peace-keeping capacity."

In tandem with *Delgam Uukw versus The Queen*, the war would be fought on the land. Wii Seeks posed for an American photographer's camera and said, "This is the last photo of Ralph Michell in peacetime." It was obviously going to be an interesting summer.

Update

*T*he landmark land claims trial of the Gitksan-Wet'suwet'en people met a solid wall of resistance at the B.C. Supreme Court. Chief Justice Allan McEachern handed down his ruling March 8, 1991, a day now known as "Black Friday" among B.C.'s aboriginal peoples. In order to rule against the Gitksan-Wet'suwet'en hereditary chiefs, McEachern had to find a way out of the clear legal path set out in recent years for aboriginal rights cases. Judge McEachern found a way. In a ruling that has shocked judges and lawyers throughout the country, the B.C. Supreme Court now holds that British Columbia's Indians, unlike any other aboriginal peoples in Canada, have no "aboriginal rights." Whatever rights aboriginal peoples enjoy under Canada's Constitution run out of steam before they get to the B.C. border because of the former British colony's peculiar history. The Gitksan-Wet'suwet'en case, known as Delgan Uukw Versus the Queen, is now before the B.C. Court of Appeal. From there, the case is expected to proceed to the Supreme Court of Canada. A final decision may take four more years.*

The Handle of Life:

The Struggle Back On The Land

by Skanu'u (Ardythe Wilson)

If we were concerned about the destruction of our territories before the Chiefs filed suit against the Province of B.C. in 1984, we were horrified by the sharp increase in logging, and the methods used, that took place from that point onward.

The ugly practices of clearcutting (cutting down all trees within a given block), and high-grading (taking only 15 to 50 percent of "marketable" trees from a clearcut), left vast chunks of the territories scarped raw. With every rainfall and spring runoff, the water of the creeks and rivers would turn a deep, muddy brown from the topsoils of the clearcuts and the loosened earth of the hastily constructed logging roads.

It was obvious that a renewed effort to protect the land was necessary if we did not want to see a barren wasteland by the time *Delgamuukw vs. The Queen* had run its course through the Canadian justice system. The Gitksan and Wet'suwet'en people geared up for another round of direct action on the land.

In an effort to minimize our struggles on the land, the companies whose corporate interests were seen to be in jeopardy and supported by the provincial government, initiated a common line of attack and dismissal of our actions. The protests and resistance of the Gitksan and We'suwet'en, they claimed, should be dismissed as newly-invented, publicity-seeking stunts to bring attention to *Delgamuukw vs. The Queen*. We knew it to be otherwise. Ask any person from a given House, and you will be told of one or more of their ancestors who took part in some form of resistance against

111

From *Colonialism On Trial* by Don Monet and Skanu'u (Ardythe Wilson), New Society Publishers, PO Box 189, Gabriola Island, BC Canada V0R 1X0. Copyright © 1992 by Skanu'u and the Gitksan Wet'suwet'en people.

Marshmallow Wars

In the summer of 1986, a SWAT team of Ministry of Fisheries officers raided fishing nets in Kitsegukla. Figuring that the next likely raid would be at Kitwanga, people quickly built a smokehouse there. When the officers arrived, they were pelted with marshmallows.

Seizure on Luulak's Land

From *Colonialism On Trial* by Don Monet and Skanu'u (Ardythe Wilson), New Society Publishers, PO Box 189, Gabriola Island, BC Canada V0R 1X0. Copyright © 1992 by Art Wilson.

the encroachment and impositions of the European.

This chapter of our history tells how we took direct action to protect ourselves, our land, and our resources from the time of earliest European contact. These specific actions are by no means the only ones we took to protect our interests, but they do offer an insight into the consistency and commitment of our people in addressing the injustices of the colonial powers.

In the early 1800s, when the first European fur-traders arrived, they were unable to infiltrate our trading and economic systems in the Northwest because they had nothing we needed or wanted that we couldn't get from our tribal neighbors. We resisted them.

When the government surveyors came to measure our reserves, we confiscated their equipment, pulled stakes from the ground and escorted them firmly out of the territory. We resisted then.

When miners negligently caused the burning of houses and poles in the village of Gitsegukls, the Chiefs and their House members protested their actions and the inactivity of the colonial government by blockading the Skeena River. When the influx of miners grew and began to occupy parts of the territories without the consent of the Houses, our people protested.

The list grew longer as the world progressed into the 20th century. Our families hid the children from missionaries and Indian agents so they would not be shipped out to residential schools; our Feasts went underground with the passing of the anti-Potlatch laws; we held secret meetings to discuss the "land question" when it became illegal for "Indians" to meet to discuss land issues; we hid family regalia to escape the burning barrels of the missionaries; Chiefs were arrested for halting road-building; women stoned federal Fisheries Officers sent to blow up a rock in Hagwilget canyon; young children suffered daily strappings from missionaries of Indian day schools for continuing to speak their own language in school.

As the forces, restrictions and impositions grew and spread throughout the territories, the Chiefs and House members necessarily grew more creative and aggressive in their resistance. We rebuilt and re-occupied fish camps to resist the restrictions of the Department of Fisheries. In Gitwangax, at the Anki Iss fish camp, women and children pelted well-armed officers with marshmallows as they attempted to break through the human blockade to seize a net from the river. In Kispiox, at the Gwin Oop fish camp, the people stepped aside and watched as a fishery officer snatched an empty cork-line from the river then, red-faced, beat a hasty retreat.

Chiefs and House members, whose nets had been seized because of their refusal to accept permits for fishing at their traditional fishing sites, marched into the fisheries office and took back their nets.

On the territories, we blockaded logging roads and set up camps in an attempt to slow down the clearcutting of timber, to ensure proper standards were maintained to protect the environment from erosion and chemicals, and to ensure that standards of road building were being adhered to. We blockaded railroads to bring a halt to the hazardous spraying of chemicals along the rail lines that were polluting the spawning grounds, berry grounds and grazing areas. A well-coordinated blockade at the Babine River was successful in keeping Westar (the logging company) and the Province from opening up the untouched northern territories of the Gitksan to logging.

As much as the governments and big business want the general public to believe that our vocal and active protests are a newly created activity, the reality is that, historically and to the present, we have been active in our resistance to be silenced and to made invisible.

The reality is that we have never given up, never sold, nor lost in battle, our ownership and jurisdiction to our territories. The reality is that our societies, our cultures and our systems are alive and well. They have sustained us through more than 150 of the darkest, most destructive years that our people have ever known and will continue to sustain us as we reassume our right to be self-sufficient, self-reliant and self-governing.

What must be, will be.

Native Language Survival

by Richard Dauenhauer & Nora Marks Dauenhauer
Sealaska Heritage Foundation

Sixteen Alaska Native languages are "at risk," according to Dr. Michael Krauss, a Native language expert at the University of Alaska. Included are Tlingit, Haida, Tsimshian, and most if not all Athapaskan languages in Alaska.

The decline of languages is not unique to Alaska. Half or more of the approximately 200 Indian languages still spoken north of Mexico are also at risk or "obsolescent" as are many of the smaller indigenous languages of the former Soviet Union, especially the Native languages of Siberia and the Far East. Finnish linguist Juha Janhunen argues that chances for survival depend not as much on total numbers of speakers as on percentage of speakers. Thus, Nganasan, a relatively isolated language of the Samoyed family with just over one thousand speakers, has excellent chances for survival because 85% of the population speaks it. In contrast, Evenki, a geographically widespread language of the Tungus family with ten thousand speakers, is in danger because only 34% of the Evenki population speak it.

Tlingit, Haida, and Tsimshian have very few speakers, and a very low percentage of speakers to total population. The 1982 estimates of speakers are Tlingit: 1,600 in Alaska, 100 in Canada; Tsimshian: 150 in Alaska, 3,500 in Canada; Haida: 100 in Alaska, 200 in Canada. These figures are now ten years old. Generous a decade ago, the current estimates of speakers are greatly reduced.

Approximately 95% of the world's Tlingit speakers live in Alaska. On the average, there are about 25 speakers in most villages. Juneau, Anchorage, and Seattle are more difficult to estimate, but the 1982 figure of 1,600 is probably now closer to 1,000. The youngest speaker of Tlingit whom we know is 40 years old. Most speakers are 60 and older. Unless current trends reverse, Tlingit will be extinct or nearly so in forty years. For all languages in the "obsolescent" category, there is no "critical mass" of speakers, and for all indigenous languages, in contrast to immigrant languages such as German or Vietnamese, there is no other homeland in which the language is spoken and to which younger generations can return to study the ancestral language and culture.

How did things get this way?

Many cultural, historical, and sociolinguistic factors contributed to the present situation, but we will focus here on schooling. Historically, the position of American education in Alaska has been one of resistance to Alaska Native languages, literature and culture in the schools. The pressure for Tlingits to assimilate began in the 1880's in Southeast Alaska, and it is important to say a few words about this before continuing. During the Russian period, bilingual education was the norm, and literacy was encouraged in Russian as well as in Native languages. But in the American period, educators insisted on policies of "English only," and expressly forbade the use or inclusion of Native languages in the schools. Partly to avoid the physical genocide of the Indian wars and the reservation system, Presbyterian missionary educators such as Sheldon Jackson and S. Hall Young argued that the Native people of Alaska should be trained so as to be useful and acceptable to whites. Assimilation was central to this; Natives had to give up traditional languages and lifestyles and replace them with English language and white American cultural values.

It is ironic that missionaries of a religion whose spiritual ancestors were burned at the stake over the issue of Bible translation should deny it in their own mission fields, arguing that Native languages should be let to die because they are ridden with sin and are inadequate to express Christian thought. While the modern Presbyterian Church no longer maintains this position, the debate is not of historical interest alone; it is still alive and well in the Juneau Christian community as of 1991, with certain fundamentalist churches arguing strongly that one cannot be Christian without renouncing all aspects of Tlingit culture.

At the 1989 annual meeting of Sealaska Corporation, a young Native woman stood up and made a very impassioned speech, saying that "Tlingit culture is an abomination in the sight of God" and that "God is punishing the Tlingit people because of their culture." She argues that drug and alcohol abuse, and family violence are "plagues on the community sent by God as punishment." This young woman is not alone in her spiritual crisis, her search for identity, and self-concept, her attempt to resolve conflict of loyalty.

Jackson and Young were not alone in their philosophy of education. In 1901, Commissioner Harris wrote in a letter to Julia Ward Howe, that

> *We have no higher calling in the world than to be missionaries of our ideas to those people who have not yet reached the Anglo-Saxon frame of mind.* (R. Dauenhauer, *Conflicting Visions in Alaskan Education*)

In a memorandum from the same period, Commissioner Harris ordered all teachers to:

> *Take with them such books of literature as portray in the most powerful form the ideas and convictions of the people of England and the United States. The work of Shakespeare, Dickens, Walter Scott and their like furnish exactly the material to inspire the teacher and to arouse and kindle the sluggish minds of the natives of Alaska with sentiments and motives of action which lead our civilization.* (Ibid.)

The connection between God, American civilization, and the English language is clearly articulated by Senator Albert Beverage on January 9, 1900, as recorded in the Congressional Record:

> *We will not renounce our part in the mission of our race, trustee, under God, of the civilization of the world...God has not been preparing the English speaking and Teutonic peoples for a thousand year for nothing...No!...and of all our race he has marked the American people as His chosen nation to finally lead in the regeneration of the world. This is the divine mission of America, and it holds for us all the profit, all the glory, and all the happiness possible to man.* (Ibid.)

117

Beverage was not an architect of education in Alaska, but his comments convey the attitude of the era. This passage is usually received by our lecture audiences with mixed reactions of laughter and dismay. Unfortunately, the social, political, and cultural impacts of this position are still felt, and the attitudes expressed by Young, Jackson, Harris, and Beverage are viable in Alaska today.

Bilingual legislation of the 1970s was met with fierce resistance by many administrators and teachers, and the anti-Native language sentiment continues in the 1990s. In 1988, high school students in a predominately Tlingit village requested us to do a workshop on our newly published book *Haa Shuká, Our Ancestors: Tlingit Oral Narratives*. A district administrator denied their request, saying "I don't see where Tlingit literature fits into our curriculum." In late 1989, the commissioner of education in Alaska (who was Alaska Native) made a strong appeal for the inclusion of Native language instruction in the schools. Most of the larger communities supported the commissioner, but, as in the 1970s, many rural superintendents rose in opposition. The Juneau newspaper (December 8, 1989) reported one superintendent as claiming that "English is virtually the only language in his district" and that the proposed policy "would require...schools to resurrect lost languages for instructional purposes." In January 1990, the superintendent of a predominantly Tlingit community in Southeast Alaska responded by letter, saying "our school board is vehemently opposed to any erosion of local authority. Our board has rejected the funding formula revenues that bicultural generates even though carving, Indian dancing, legends and stories and beading are extended to the children and community at various times as extra curricular events."

"Local control" is the argument used to justify the exclusion of Tlingit humanities content from the curriculum. When the situation is viewed historically and in the present, a definite anti-Native pattern emerges. Nowhere is it suggested that God is opposed to English, or that English language, literacy and literature should be excluded from the schools and taught exclusively at home. In 1990, we enter the second decade of the second century of suppression.

This system of education, into which all Native children were drawn by force of law, severely impacted Alaska Native personality and transmission of languages. Government boarding schools were in operation into the 1970s, and several generations of Alaska Native people were educated under the "English-only" policies. The enduring message of the system was "You're the wrong color, you speak the wrong language, you have the wrong culture, you have the wrong religion." Even in the case of the Aleuts, who were already Christian and literate, it was the wrong church (Orthodox) and the wrong alphabet (Cyrillic). After one hundred years of this policy, administrators and school boards continue to debate the wisdom of including Alaska Native languages, literature, and culture in the curriculum. Bilingual education is always an emotional issue in the United States, and the controversy continues in Alaska. As this essay is being written in February of 1992, the issue of including or requiring Native languages in schools is under consideration in the Alaska State legislature. According to the Alaska Department of Education, 63 schools in the state with Native-majority enrollment offer no Native language classes. In the meantime, the same educators who debate whether Native language and literature merit inclusion in the academic canon seriously ponder the origins of "low self esteem" and high drop-out rates of Native students. We agree with Krauss, who writes in *Alaska Native Languages: Past, Present, and Future*:

> *I view the obliteration of Alaskan Native Languages by English as an unnecessary final tragic chapter in the continuing conflict in American History, the "winning of the West." The physical genocides of the nineteenth century were replaced in the twentieth by cultural genocide in the classroom: "Cowboys and Indians" moved into the schools, and extermination and removal were replaced by assimilation.*

What is it like when a language dies?

Because it is always haunted by the specter of death, the study of oral literature and indigenous languages around the world is far more emotional than any aspect of written literature. If the German language dies out in an immigrant family in the United States, any interested descendant can study it in high school or college, or can go to Germany, Austria, or Switzerland where the language is alive and well. But if a Native American language dies, there is no place on earth one can travel to learn it. The public statements that some school administrators continue to make in opposition to teaching Alaska Native languages would not be tolerated if made about some endangered species of bird or snail. The impending death of a language, like one's own death, or the death of a loved one, is often uncomfortable to contemplate.

One of the most eloquent descriptions of grief over the loss of language and culture is Anna Nelson Harry's "Lament for Eyak." Anna was among the last three speakers of Eyak, and its last tradition bearer. Krauss worked with Anna in the 1960s and early 1970s, collecting texts and compiling an Eyak dictionary. The Eyak language is now virtually extinct, but, thanks to the efforts of Krauss, and the energy, intelligence, and good will of Anna Nelson Harry and the three or four other Eyak speakers still alive at the time, it is well documented and a bilingual edition of oral tradition by Anna survives, from which excerpts of her "Lament" are taken. (*In Honor of Eyak: The Art of Anna Nelson Harry.* Michael Krauss. Fairbanks: Alaska Native Language Center, University of Alaska.)

> .../ *All alone here I'll go around.* / *Like Ravens I'll live alone.* / *My aunts are dying off on me and alone I'll be living.* /.../ *My uncles also have all died out on me and I can't forget them.* / *After my uncles all died off,* / *my aunts are dying off next.* / *I'm all alone.* / *With some children I survive,* / *on this earth.* /.../ *Where will I go next?* / *Wherever will I go next?* / *They are already all extinct.* / *They have been wiped out.* /.../ *Why is it I alone,* / *just I alone have survived?* / *I survive..*

What can we do about it?

In the late 1960s, Nora Marks Dauenhauer began working with Tlingit counterparts of Anna Nelson Harry. Richard Dauenhauer came to the work a few years later, from a different direction. The ground rules for our teamwork were established over twenty years ago by the elders, who insisted that it be done from a Tlingit point of view, and in a way acceptable to the oral tradition bearers and the Tlingit community. At that time, the majority of elders were skeptical of and often opposed to books. On the one hand, most of them wanted their words to survive, but they complained that the way Tlingit was usually presented in books omitted everything that was important to them as tradition bearers, so that there was nothing left of the Tlingit oral literature. They specifically objected to "generic" stories in paraphrased or rewritten English, often simplified or edited into children's versions, with no credit given to the story teller and the owning clan. The elders were very sensitive to the style of such rewrites, and would comment, "That's not the story I told." The elders were reacting negatively because the aesthetics and "rules" of oral style, content, and context had been abandoned in favor of literary aesthetics.

Our challenge was to document Tlingit oral literature in written versions, but with style and content acceptable to the tradition bearers. The easiest way to do this was to write down exactly what the elders said, and read it back to them for verification. We began a story where the narrator started it, and ended where he or she ended. This may seem simple enough, but it was a revolutionary step in writing of Tlingit literature. Story tellers usually begin with what we call a "narrative frame" in which they somehow identify themselves, the clan owning "oral copyright" to the material, and their right to transmit through genealogy and training. While some kind of narrative frame is almost always included in oral performance, they almost never appear in English rewrites. Also, the individual story tellers and their clans are usually not acknowledged, especially in the composite, "generic," popular rewrites based on older ethnographies. This may reflect the popular fallacy that folklore is "anonymous."

We were also interested in "oral literary criticism" — in what the tradition bearers themselves think about the material, what it means in their lives, and how their lives have shaped the oral literature. We realize that there is a major critical debate in literature over the extent to which writers can be trusted to understand and interpret their own creative work in a rational and conceptual manner, and that the same debate can probably be extended to oral literature, but it seemed reasonable to at least ask tradition bearers about the meaning of their work.

All told, the following became our guidelines for the last twenty years: to feature identifiable elders in a specific performance; to transcribe their words in Tlingit; to translate into English with attention to the style of the original; to treat the oral literature as serious, adult literature; to respect the Tlingit point of view from which it is presented; and, through annotations and introductions, to help establish and explain the cultural context of the original, making explicit knowledge that may be assumed by the tradition bearer in speaking to the fieldworker, but not evident to the reader. It is also important to note the dual role of Nora Marks Dauenhauer in this: as a native speaker of Tlingit raised in a traditional family she shared in the elders' concerns with such conviction that she could both insist on the guidelines and implement them as a researcher.

121

In addition to working with oral literature, we also develop instructional materials such as pedagogical grammars and glossaries. Linguists emphasize that for Tlingit, Haida, and Tsimshian there is no "hearth," there is no "market place." They mean that for a language to survive as a natural, living language, there must be either a home or a community setting for it — a hearth or market place. None exist for Tlingit, Haida, or Tsimshian. Part of the challenge of language teaching is to create such a situation — perhaps by teaching to family groups in community settings rather than in the conventional classroom segregated by age; perhaps at summer camps or other intensive, immersion settings. But unless we develop alternatives to schools (as conventionally constituted) for the teaching of Native language and literature, we will surely lose them.

It is almost certain that the languages of Southeast Alaska will not survive as spoken languages for all situations. But the languages can survive in selected cultural contexts, such as song and dance, visual art, and perhaps ceremonial use. At Sealaska Heritage Foundation efforts are aimed toward increased awareness of the problem and toward restoration to whatever extent possible, accompanied by increased personal and community mental well-being.

"Language and Cultural Preservation" is a phrase commonly used to describe such efforts. But "preservation" is an ambiguous term. Talking about "preservation" is like talking about fish and berries. Do we envision a thriving berry patch or jam? An enduring salmon run or canned salmon? By "language preservation" do we refer to the living ecosystem or to home preserves? Organizations can preserve language and literature in written and recorded form. Organizations, linguists, and folklorists can document traditions and produce instructional materials and cultural resource materials, but only individuals and communities can preserve a spoken language or maintain a living tradition.

INTERVIEW WITH TESS GALLAGHER

by TERRI LEE GRELL

Tess Gallagher describes herself as "kind of a ptarmigan of a poet" when she is writing. Ptarmigans live at the top of alpine mountains and are completely tame when one happens upon them because no one goes there. Gallagher's "alpine mountain" is a small house on a promontory just outside of Port Angeles, Washington, a house dominated by windows and light, with a sweeping view of the Strait of Juan de Fuca. It is the house she and Raymond Carver built as a writing retreat and romantic hideaway. Though devastated by Carver's death from cancer in 1988, Gallagher returned to writing and recently had two new collection published, Moon Crossing Bridge and Portable Kisses. Moon Crossing Bridge is a journey through mourning and the new belongings and recognitions such loss of a life's companion and love allows. Portable Kisses is the continuation of the light and resolve which was begun near the conclusion of Moon Crossing Bridge. Gallagher's temperament, humor and wit are present again. Though she is a ptarmigan about her physical and spiritual habitat, Gallagher's writing, spanning two decades, one collection of essays, one of short stories and a screenplay with Raymond Carver, is bold and spirited and often punctuated with a sting. "I aim for the spine," she says of her intent. "I want you to feel a little chill when you finish a poem of mine."

TERRI LEE GRELL: Sky House…it's very comfortable here.

TESS GALLAGHER: Just right for one or two quiet people who get along well. I call it my hideout. I named it Sky House because the people across the way built a house that blocked the view of the town where I was born. [Port Angeles] Very tall, large house built on a small lot, took the view away from another couple on this road, too. I thought I should name the house to protect it from further encroachment.

TL: That reminds me of something you wrote about a woman who brings the issue of "encroachment" into poetry. You said in your essay on Marianne Moore,[§] one reason you admire her work is her poems about animals on the verge of extinction. You pointed out the way she brought attention to the issue, to protect endangered forms from further encroachment, to preserve them.

Tess: Yes, even before it became popular to do that, Moore was doing it.

TL: Do poets today feel that poetry itself is an endangered "species," and so there is more poetry being written *about* poetry, or about writing poetry, or about being a poet?

Tess: There has always been that element even since I started writing. When I went to writers' workshops I remember there being a lot of complaints that poems coming up in the workshop were self-referential. They would be a kind of human cry. But I think it's a natural thing for a poem to do, to talk of how it is happening, about its mechanism. Of course, if it gets too self-reflective we won't be interested.

It seems like now I'm asked more and more to speak to people who I thought weren't very interested in poetry, and I'm finding that they are writing poems and reading them. Last year, for instance, I was with doctors attending the Institute of Literature and Medicine at Hiram College near Cleveland. They used literature to explore different aspects of aging and illness, and stages of loss. I hadn't been aware of this institute before. Then I spoke at the Separation and Loss Institute at Virginia Mason Clinic in Seattle, and I was amazed. I was a keynote speaker and I'm a *poet!* Quite a wonderful invitation. There was another poet there, Ann Pitkin, and she happens to be a psychotherapist. I have a psychotherapist friend in Montreal who uses poetry in her work. I met a doctor at the Hiram College Institute who encourages the reading and writing of poetry in his practice.

TL: So you're saying poetry is definitely not dead, or even threatened.

Tess: No, I don't believe so. Not as I experience it.

TL: We've both read the article by Dana Gioia.[‡] I got the impression from the article that this "poetry is dying" issue has been going on since at least 1934, when, as Gioia points out, Edmund Wilson published his essay, "Is Verse a Dying Technique?" The fact that the debate has been going

---

[§] "Throwing the Scarecrows from the Garden: The Poetry of Marianne Moore;" *A Concert of Tenses: Essays on Poetry* by Tess Gallagher, 1986, University of Michigan Press.

[‡] "Can Poetry Matter?", The Atlantic Monthly, May 1991.

on this long in itself tells us something of the staying power of poetry!

Tess: Yes. Gioia makes the claim that poetry's influence has "eroded." But then he says something I find is contradictory; that 20,000 poets are coming out of these writing programs in the next ten years.

TL: But I think Gioia means 20,000 poets out of a job.

Tess: But he doesn't say that. Gioia says that we haven't seen the effects of the influence of poetry in the communities. But my experience has been very different from his, because I live in a village, as such, not an urban area, and I have watched for forty years what is happening with poetry in this town. The community's attitude is very different now about poetry than when I grew up here. There are now poetry events at the community college and a Fine Arts Center, attended by people from all walks of life. If you go there for one of the noon readings, there are people there on their lunch breaks, from the community. Of course, this being a community college, the focus is different than at a university. It depends on students coming from the community, people who are working and take classes. I can't disqualify their interest in poetry simply because they're at a community college. Here, and in other communities, it is a center where people can gather. Also, Gioia didn't acknowledge all the work being done in the prisons. Poets have been teaching and reading in the prisons for the past twenty years. He didn't acknowledge that in small communities poets often work with the elderly, and poets are asked by local organizations to give programs, to give eulogies at funerals, to dedicate libraries, to speak at teachers' strikes — all things I've done. I don't know that we have a huge amount of stature, but we are not unnoticed. I mean, nobody rushes up to me in the supermarket! But people are very much aware and proud that I live here.

TL: I have heard poetry in a hundred different places, but never have I gone to a university sponsored reading. I wondered where Gioia goes to hear poetry.

Tess: I'm not anti-university anymore, though I had been for many years. But Gioia seems to think universities support poetry better than they do, whereas I feel entirely expendable within that structure. Sure enough, when I left, the waters closed over with hardly a trace. I'm in touch with a lot of my former students, and they have a hard struggle. The time when universities were able to accommodate all of those who wanted to teach writing is certainly past. Young poets are going to have to be more versatile. They can't come up out of those writing programs assuming they will go get cushy university jobs. They're going to have to get out. You know, travel and see the world! I went to Ireland because I was curious about meeting those poets and getting in touch with a culture in which poetry was appreciated and acknowledged by "the folk." If you went into a pub and you said you were a poet, you wouldn't be laughed out of existence, you'd be asked to recite one of your poems. Poets do need to volunteer themselves in other places. Anytime that you work in a community you have the opportunity to share your writing with others. To give poetry to the people around you.

TL: So what part of this argument, that poetry is in danger of losing its influence, can we take seriously?

Terri: It's true, in universities, that poets are the primary audience for readings. And it's true what Gioia says about poetry magazines. They haven't made an effort to find readers other than poets and students. They will have to really exert themselves to create that kind of reception for their magazines.

TL: I agree with Gioia on at least one count; that leading critics rarely review poetry, and that "virtually no one reviews it except other poets."

Tess: Yes. Absolutely. I think there needs to be a lot more reviewing of poetry, and not only poetry, but of literary magazines. I think it would be interesting if poetry magazines were reviewed issue by issue somewhere. I would like to see individual issues reviewed. There's lots of room for a literary journal which would do just that. I think another legitimate complaint that Gioia said was about *The New York Times Book Review.* Poetry books are reviewed in groups, and you will have a poet who has been writing for twenty years reviewed with someone who has a first book, and there's no differentiation made whatsoever. One of my books was reviewed along with a couple of early books by other writers. Why do other poets agree to do this? I think poets ought to write en masse to *The New York Times Book Review* about the situation. If people started to complain regularly or found some organized way to do it, through the Writers' Union, the AWP or the American Poetry Society, then possibly it could be changed. I don't think that small press publishers have put enough pressure on *The New York Times.* They don't know how to motivate that arena yet.

TL: What signs do you see that poetry will continue to invigorate our culture?

Tess: Poetry and art are being taught in our primary schools. That wasn't happening when I was growing up in these same schools. I never saw a poet until I was 17 years old and went to University of Washington and met Theodore Roethke. Now there are poets reading every week in my town;

loggers, grocery clerks, secretaries, lawyers and retired people from all sorts of professions participate in these readings. As far as poetry's spiritual influence, I have people writing to me every week about Raymond Carver's work. I met a man by Ray's graveside, on the first anniversary of Ray's death. He was with two friends and we stood there and talked. He told me had found Ray's book, *A New Path to the Waterfall*, in the "inspirational" section of his local Boston bookstore! People have written to me and talked quite a lot about the impact of that book. One man who was facing death from cancer called me from Seattle. Someone had given him the book as a mainstay in his last days. We had this incredible hour-long conversation, and then, after his death, his wife also called me to say she'd found strength from the book. There are many instances of this in my own life that leads me to believe that poetry still has a powerful spiritual influence. Perhaps it isn't as pervasive or as evangelical as say, the Baptists. Maybe it doesn't provoke instant hypnosis like MTV, but it's there. It's present.

TL: You've just written two new collections and these are the first you've written since Ray's death. It seems you've found strength in poetry.

Tess: They seem more like provisional rafts I've thrown together out of the debris of my situations. When I've been most devastated by life I've fallen entirely silent, as I did the first six months after Ray's death. Poems could have nothing to do there in the abyss. Also I had charge of Ray's own last book of poems and those poems had to be brought to publication.

In January of 1989 I did write "Red Poppy" — the first poem of any consequences after his death. Other poems began to come, expressions of those actual days and feelings I lived through in this afterwards. I was strong enough finally to revisit the last times we had together, and the dying itself, the things I did to stay close to his spirit, since death leaves that for us. I wrote these poems in Sky House.

Like someone who names a house Sky House, I'm always looking for actual ways to extend my enclosures — my houses, my poems, my lost loves — by noticing the larger space which contains me — sky. Hard not to be hopeful with that over you, right?

127

Ee cud Sayve Weert...

by Paul Pintarich

In Portland a few years ago, I asked author Kurt Vonnegut about the future of the world; whether or not he thought we might survive.

Lighting another link in a long chain of cigarettes smoked through that afternoon, Vonnegut cut his bleary basset eyes and asked if I had read his last book.

Nodding after I said yes, he then puffed deeply before exhaling a cloud of cynicism out from what must be totally ruined lungs.

"Then you remember the inscription I suggested be carved into a canyon wall by the last people on earth: 'We could have saved it but we were too lazy and greedy to care.'"

I remember, I think of it often, it bothers me; but more, I wonder what travelers from the outer reaches of the universe will think when they arrive and see: "Ee cud sayve weert nocre greedle weezly arcre but."

"Gimme that gudam chizel! Yukon ried fourshits aik!"

PhuckingAk!

For we are living in a country too lazy to read and too greedy to care about much except getting in cars and going to malls and getting things; in coming home with our things, then sitting in front of things, watching things, hearing things and eating things, until we become things who can't think abut things anymore.

Take your BMWs, for example. It is the Great American Dream right now to have a "Beamer," particularly one with a sun roof and a telephone. It means that you can look good calling someone, while at the same time risking your life trying to negotiate a corner with one hand.

Yet has anyone come to realize that the BMW transmission emits a high-pitched whine that can only be heard by Weimaraner dogs and Yuppies? That over time its sympathetic vibrations penetrate the skull and render numb all but those brain cells responsive to suggestions for places to do lunch or babblings from or about Madonna?

I don't think so. In the world we have today, drugged for so long by television, sleepwalking through an overweight, increasingly self-indulgent wasteland on a life journey that leads only to death or Disneyland, guided by the sound bites of banality, there are few thinkers anymore.

F. Scott Fitzgerald, in a 1992 letter to Ernest Hemingway, might well write: "Dear Ernie: Loved the galleys, but I would like to talk to you a little bit more about the plot development in 'The Sun Also Rises.' I really don't think you intended to have Jake Barnes lose his…"

And Papa's reply: "Dear Scottie: Balls! I haven't the time to read anymore. Give me a call."

"The Collected Phone Calls of F. Scott and Ernest."

Sound bites, sight bites, little bitty bites of nothing is what we have become. Our politics, our culture, our literature, our traditions, our environment, all are being sacrificed through the pervasive panderings of the electronic media.

So what does all this have to do with my job as a book reviewer on a daily metropolitan newspaper? Nothing perhaps, because, as our advertising department polls reveal, most of you won't have read this far anyway.

It's not anyone's fault, of course, it's just that no one has the time. I'm sorry, I should end this right here and not even bother to remind people that in the Old Days (that's right, just take it), men and women worked fourteen to sixteen hours a day, milked cows, hauled coal, walked to school through snow up to their ass, ate poor food and studied by the light of candles, gas lights, and kerosene lamps.

It was all Charles Dickens' country around here then, with a bit of Kafka thrown in.

Yet these same people read, wrote manifestos, fomented revolutions, thought for themselves, and were thinner besides. People walked or rode streetcars and the air and water were cleaner.

If people wanted to know something they read up on it; if they wanted to dream or feel poetry in their soul, they read; the Bible was a book, after all, and it is God's "Word," not the Sound Bites of God.

When I was in the first grade I saw Spot run. But by then I had already seen Superman fly, and knew why, while most of my contemporaries were capable of reading Donald Duck and knew that those great big books on philosophy were not about Mickey Mouse's dog.

Comic books; why not? Then Little Big Books, then Classic Comics, then Edgar Allen Poe, then science fiction, then Ernest Hemingway; now, I'm telling you things have changed and it's scary.

But just how scary? Well, it can be unbelievable.

With a few notable exceptions, newspapers hardly acknowledge books anymore; in fact, an editor of mine who proclaims somewhat proudly that she is from the "text is dead generation," frequently placates my laments by saying, "Don't worry. No one reads anymore."

Another editor, while I was acknowledging the 100th anniversary of the birth of J.R.R. Tolkien, creator of "The Hobbit," was unable to link the author with his creation. At the same time, I was asked if my rather modestly-lengthed story on Tolkien might be broken down into three parts, "...So we don't lose the readers."

I could go on, reciting horror stories that might be epitomized by an inquiry, some time ago, from an assistant Sunday magazine editor who, having been told that the book I was reviewing was a novel, then asked, "Is it fiction?"

My replies, or arguments as they have become more often, express a concern for the future. And too often, I'm afraid, I must appear to be an aging curmudgeon — I prefer "craggy, middle-aged man" — among the now younger panderers of hip, slick, and cool.

It should be noted that newspapers acknowledge they are publishing a product for people who have little or no desire to read. At least among the advertising "target group," which is women and young people ages 20 something to about 40.

Everyone else, I'm sorry to say, is on their own. If you are 40 and above, that group, according to the American Booksellers Association, which reads most of the books that are worthwhile, then you're out of luck.

Week after week, thinking human beings, people who, by the way, still read newspapers, must suffer through shorter and shorter columns on funky rock groups, trend setters, rumors, gossip, whether or not to wear red galoshes, "Streets of Dreams," and descriptions of the garage where Madonna keeps her BMW.

Most of these famous and infamous, whose career expectancies seldom exceed that of the mayfly, appear at one time or another in a photograph featured in the upper left-hand corner of the front page — known as the "Vanna Box" — so that the devoted might realize, "Hey! These old newspaper guys are hip after all."

Once, when John Updike was arriving for the Portland Arts & Lectures Series, I suggested his likeness might be a nice change in the "Vanna Box," but was told, "No one will know who he is."

Too true, sadly, though my reply was, "Well, then, why don't we tell them?"

Because no one reads anymore.

So we have a book page that is not a full page, and news of poets and writers and publishers, which abound in the Northwest, a region currently building one of the richest literary traditions in the land, often gets neglected simply because of a lack of space.

Unfortunately for all of us, newspapers can't be blamed entirely for that is a major cultural transition. Always dependent on advertising, and certainly not a literary quarterly, the traditional daily newspaper has been rumpled badly by exigencies of survival in an age of electronic competition.

And let's face it, paper costs are up, and if we want to get paid, us print journalists, we should be grateful for the bright shiny glut of colored advertisements that give the Sunday paper its capacious girth.

Yet there is an inexorable self-destructive quality to all of this. As we pander more and more to the demands of advertisers who may or may not know (or are trying to persuade) popular taste, we become locked in a wasteful dialectic determined by definitions of mediocrity.

Again, what does this have to do with being a book editor? Plenty, for if one is responsible in the job, not simply as a flak for those books that are immediate bestsellers, their authors made famous not for their writing skills, but simply because of the money they have made, then we become consumer advocates in support of good thinking.

As essayists and critics, we should provide more than "book reports," for readers deserve opportunities to enjoy the realizations of Descartes, undeterred by shallow pronouncements from those who claim the novel is dead, books are dying, and who find reading a bore.

Now listen up. If you don't read, your imagination is not sustained and many solutions to the problems of the world are not at hand. Each week I get scores of books on the environment, on safe sex, on world history, economics, politics, literature, biographies; on space and global warming and alternatives to fucking up the world just to have more malls and cars and stuff.

Often, there is a sudden and terrible realization that the only people reading these books are people who already care; like poets whose books are only read by other poets.

And consider this: if we are not familiar with words and what they mean; if sentences and metaphors and subtleties and nuances and symbols and allegories and themes and references, and what have you, are ignored and left to disappear, then the texture and richness of all that we consider culture (Yes, even the fun, trashy stuff), is meaningless.

If there is a rock group, "Steppenwolf" or "Led Zeppelin," for example, then one certainly needs a reference to Herman Hesse's existential novel; and knowledge of those mammoth lighter-than-air craft is required if that joke is to succeed.

And, of course, readers need a modicum of intellectual perception if they are to read the newspapers. As standards are lowered to bring in the advertising dollars, we all suffer, for the cultural constituency of the country becomes disenfranchised, our children don't learn anything, voters become overfed dolts suckled by television into an aspic of ennui and, eventually, things begin to crumble, as they are now.

After the newspapers fold, ironically, because they have helped create a populace no longer able to read them, then we all close up shop, head home, and crash on the couch to eat Cheetos and watch the Simpsons.

I consider my job on a par with those who were braiding buggy whips at the turn of the century. It's difficult for me to believe, at age fifty three, that I'd live to see a world where dreams, curiosity and imagination are being systematically sublimated in deference to endlessly cliche', twittery gossip about Bozos we must constantly endure in our tabloid society.

Often I tell people, "Read 'War and Peace.' Go ahead, read the sonofabitch. Read 'Moby Dick,' read Wallace Stegner, Annie Dillard, Jane Austen, James Jones, Hemingway by all means, but just read *something*, for Chrissake!"

And too often I hear, "It's too long...It's too difficult...I haven't the time..." This from people I work with, professional journalists whose work is the written word.

Bread and circuses; everyone who goes to college must read at least one book, even if they are to go immediately to Wall Street and start screwing people out of their money, which is part of the Great American Dream, along with owning a BMW and watching Madonna.

But I won't stop, for like a penguin on an ice flow drifting north, as my limits are restricted, I will shout louder: "You dumb bastards, get off your butts, turn off the television, read what I tell you to and think about something!"

If not, it will all be over, my job and yours; the world. And it won't matter anymore; you can carve the last message on the wall of the canyon: "Udumsh its bheturr eedWar Renpiece!"

Driving One Hundred

We went, in 1956,
in Sarah's boyfriend's car
out on the new highway south of Coos Bay,
toward Millington, named for a mill,
and the shinglehouse slough,
where years later someone's father's ashes
would be scattered, his last wish.
We went in Sarah's boyfriend's car,
a black convertible,
and she, wishing to try on speed,
drove fast, fast, faster,
pushing the speedometer to sixty,
seventy, eighty, as we screamed
and laughed and held ourselves down
in the seats without seatbelts.
Our hair in the wind lashed us
like something breaking over a waterfall,
and afraid our young meat and bones
would be scattered,
we screamed at Sarah, slow down slow down,
Sarah, and then she did ninety
laughing, "He'll kill me if he ever finds out,
you guys, don't tell," and pushed the pedal
down and held it, as we went fast, and faster,
screaming and dying and laughing at Sarah,
until the needle stood at one hundred,
and Sarah relented, and we
chided her then,
and began to breathe again,
at sixty, fifty, forty,
did a U at twenty,
turned around at the cutoff to Coquille.
"I almost died," we all said.
"I'll never do that again."
And our flesh settled down to go on living
as we secretly thanked her, like a goddess,
for the terrible experience.

by BARBARA DRAKE

WHAT DO STARS EAT?
THE DESIRE FOR EXTINCTION

by Lynda Sexson

Yet the absence of imagination had
Itself to be imagined.
— Wallace Stevens

We love death. It's a wonder the earth still spins, we are so fond of nothingness. To be human we must be able to imagine ourselves extinguished; conversely, to be human we must be able to imagine our continuation. This double strand of consciousness, which enables both the concepts of past and of future, both love and art, both making pickles and planting seeds, resides in the encounter with nothingness, with our love of death. We are so accustomed to myths (sacred stories) of extinction, that we are not as practiced at imagining that greater gap — continuation.

We are fond of the vanished. We love to celebrate death, what was and cannot be again. Perhaps more than any other notions of space and time, our imaginations dwell on reveries of ourselves missing. Remember the story of the dog of Pompeii? The dog, a dried corpse of devotion and intention with the petrified raisin cake in its mouth, stopped in its hurry to get back to the child, all suspended by the eruption of Mt. Vesuvius. Why is that story as compelling as Cinderella and her slipper and prince? We love, too, the dinosaurs who bequeathed their skeletons and footprints. Every five-year-old can name and distinguish the brontosaurus and the tyrannosaurus rex, those bones of forever. Kiwis and dodos, perhaps the condor, falling stars, the Taino, the Library of Alexandria, the Harappu peoples, all the cherished images of the extinguished. We love especially the extinctions of the never were, Atlanteans and griffins.

Would the earth or our existence on it be at such peril if we did not harbor a profound desire for extinction? "They lie down, they cannot rise, they are extinguished, quenched like a wick," resonates Isaiah. The crisis of Western culture is ecological. The source of that crisis is in Western culture's own version of reality: the myth of the urge to eradicate: earth and images of earth, body and song. Where does this *Contemptus Mundi* originate?

Yes, we are midwifing condor eggs and counting the elephants. We have a deep impulse, too, to continue the generations of the earth. And, there are plenty of nick-of-time recoveries in Genesis, that book of beginnings and ends, the book of risky continuation: Lot's daughters, thinking they are the last people on earth, get Lot drunk and get themselves pregnant; Tamar, waiting for years for a child, disguises herself as a prostitute to trick the seed from her father-in-law. But each of these rescues superseding even the great taboos, bring back the earth with a shadow, a sorrow. The Tower of Babel falls, and all of us fall into misunderstanding, into different tongues; the Ark sails, rescuing two-by-two, but upon landing, Noah plants a vineyard, gets drunk from his first harvest and exposes himself; the son who sees his father's nakedness is cursed. The prophets of the Hebrew scriptures bring us to the brink over and over, "As the shepherd rescues from the mouth of the lion two legs, or a piece of an ear," so shall the people be rescued, "with the corner of a couch and part of a bed." This ancient sensibility hazards transgressions as great as incest to recover the earth, but insists, too, that the peopling of the earth is tainted, that all those other tribes are engendered from ancient risky business. And in these Genesis stories is a double dream: the earth, ourselves, must continue, but at the price of the shame of our embodiment, of sexuality, of earthly life itself.

These traditional stories and impulses in which the world is cleansed and renewed, in which civilization gets revived, came under an influence of radical dualism when the Israelites were taken into exile and met up with Persian liberators and Persian metaphysics. In that Persian worldview there is a cosmic split between nature and spirit, earth and heaven, dark and light, good and evil. Theologies which developed after the exilic period were marked by a pessimism about life on earth, a desire to radically transform this world to a "perfected" spiritual plane. Christianity was formed in that apocalyptic, dualistic world. Islam, too, was formed under the influence of an apocalyptic desire for another, spiritual realm. These three great Western traditions (Judaism, Christianity, and Islam) in some part claim a sacred desire to purge themselves of the mundane. Christianity in particular, was formed in the midst of a frenzy for dividing reality in two and discarding the fleshly parts. In the process of secularization, even in a renaissance and scientific interest in the particulars of this world, Western culture clings, unconsciously, to a despising of the carnal, the ephemeral, the environment and its inhabitants. Western culture came to declare not, "Behold, it is good," but rather, "the sun will be darkened, and the moon will not give its light, and the stars will be falling from heaven."

These religions bequeathed a sensibility of self: a definition of personhood apart from family, uneasy with the body, over-against "others," separated from "nature," and alienated from the divine. It is not surprising that "nature" was the convenient embodying metaphor for all which was designated as other. All that was labeled "other," was figured as "natural," whether innocent or malevolent, was lower on the metaphysical scale and trap for those who were climbing upwards. Yet, these traditions are surrounded by worldviews of stars as alive, body as soul. Particularly when one view of reality confronts another, there are long and bloody records of the desire to exterminate the projected "other."

We know too well the story of America, the story which combines both the contempt for nature along with the role of the shepherd responsible for the straying sheep, the natural. My colleague Tom Wessel gave me a book by a nineteenth-century missionary who was sent to the "heathen" of the Western reaches of this continent, "...as the buffalo and other large animals were being exterminated, and that by starting a model farm the Indians would be attracted to it. Then schools could be started for the children, and a regular system of religious instruction could be carried on for all." The missionary, the Reverend Hines, understood the relationship between "culture" and "nature," that the buffalo, the schoolbooks, farming, and salvation were all of a piece, the shuffling of one affects the others. The missionary recounted his long association with a back-slider, Yellow Bear. The missionary took advantage of the death of Yellow Bear's wife to coerce not only Yellow Bear's promise of reform, but also the destruction of his ceremonial objects.

A photograph records the occasion of Yellow Bear casting sacred his sacred relics in the consuming fire one by one, while the gathered witnesses sang 'Ring the Bells of Heaven.' "The poor old fellow," the earnest missionary wrote, "joined in singing the hymn as best he could, but his emotions would get the better of him, and he lost control of his voice. We finished the hymn with the old man leaning upon my shoulder weeping, and catching at a word or two of the hymn when he could control his feelings."

Extermination was intertwined on many planes at once in the Reverend Hines' story. Tallying the massacres we see at a glance, we find: 1. the destruction of the buffalo, the ritual and economic base of the Plains peoples; 2. then as now, the replacement of a less invasive tradition with farming which imported agricultural "products" and methods of production — still a controversial project in the arid west — which endangers indigenous plant and animal life, water as well as people; 3. education, sometimes a euphemism for indoctrination by shame and punishment in order to eradicate another culture; 4. the destruction of material culture, particularly those ritualized objects and places, as those holy to Yellow Bear; 5. the teaching of new songs, the replacement of one ritual activity and "text" with another, as the changing of language is the changing of mind; 6. not only text, but as this hymn implies, "Ring the Bells of Heaven," is one with a particular eschatological content of a "Heaven" which belongs to a theology which seeks to overcome the Earth itself; 7. Native Americans are, in the good Reverend Hines' book, diminished to children, "children of nature"; 8. and "nature" is personified as an inferior teacher who does not know Christ; and 9. a radical dualism which the minister projected onto his objects of salvation: "They also knew from personal observation, as well as from personal experience, that there was another powerful force at work in their hearts and in the world, whose tendency was towards evil . . .and in their untutored minds they regarded them both as objects of worship." The Reverend Hines' struggle for Yellow Bear's immortal soul is a particularization, a dramatization, of how myth engenders history. With another view of nature, another myth, the invaders would have seen differently and behaved differently; they would not have so easily designated the misnamed "Indians" to the opposing side — the natural side — of their radical dualism.

Our Western past tells a story in which we desire to eradicate, not simply *otherness*, but it is *self* which we want to extinguish. Despite the Renaissance, the Enlightenment, and pluralistic secularization (these — on the surface — demythologizing movements), Western consciousness still longs to extinguish itself, desires to fly into the flames. We see the smoke curling from our own papery wings.

There are worldviews, contrary to the Western imagination, which can imagine reality without the apocalyptic. Taoists see the natural world and spiritual world as one, the natural as spontaneous, humble, and harmonious. The great Taoist philosopher Chuang-tzu confounded his listeners by asserting the Tao (ultimate reality, akin to what westerners call God) is in everything, even the tile of the floor, even the shit which is on the tile. Buddhists, from their Hindu sources, have reverence for life, *ahimsa*, will do no harm, and when they extinguish the world, they do not make for themselves an eternal picnic ground for the ego, called Heaven. Without heaven, without consciousness, the extinguish the candle, realize *nirvana*. In one of the Buddha's many lifetimes, he lay down before a starving mother tiger, giving up his flesh for the sake of the little ones, the kittens. The West, too, has a fine sense of harmony, of self-sacrifice. Why has it developed toward the annihilation of the planet? The planet, for the Western mind, is to be escaped, time itself is to be transformed. Unlike Buddhism, or its mother, Hinduism, in which the universe is *lila*, the play of the divine, popular religion in the West sees nature as "real," and has often personified nature as enemy.

In the medieval world God could get a mortal's attention by giving her a peek at Heaven. Everywhere the Medieval eye gazed, the vision was not of the earth but of the earth as a book, an allegory for the spiritual. Those medieval catalogues and mirrors showed a world in which pelicans tore open their own breasts to feed their young and thus were emblems of Christ; it was a world in which bear cubs were born as indistinct lumps, the mother licked them into bear shape, just as God's loving attention changes the amorphous clay of humanity into imitations of divine form.

The Renaissance was that time when the gaze shifted, when mortals were distracted by peeking all day at the wonders of the earth and all night by the extravagances of their dreams. The world became not an emblem or a reminder so much as an expression of human will and discovery. The Renaissance imagination stretched to the corners of the cosmos and claimed the expanse was a diagram of human life. It put things in perspective, shed light, and depicted the curl of a leaf.

The Reformation took such care to cleanse humanity of "idolatry" (of finding divine meaning in artistic or natural objects) that the startling claim was that humans could look upon the earth and find no meaning, find nothing there, and named that blankness wasteland, wilderness, vast expanse, nothing. In the rush to burn carved saints and shatter stained glass, the iconoclast insisted that the image of Christ should go, so a crucifixion was painted out, and Christ hanging between two thieves became a landscape with two crucified thieves.

It took a long time for land to appear in the Western imagination. It took a long time for us to reduce it to postcards. Western civilization is of course, made up of these medieval, Renaissance, and Reformationist ideals;

thus "nature" remains medieval, an allegory (either for the demonic or the heavenly); it remains Renaissance, something to be conquered (for science or for wealth) to create a grander image of the human; or it remains Reformationist, resulting in a nature which is severed from the divine and severed from our curiosity. These interwoven strands still make up a large part of the Western secular world view and result in a meaningless land there which is for exploitation disconnected with ultimate reality, unless for convenience, that secular world wishes to play upon the inherited dualism and justify, by divine right, its exploitation. And this is one part of that death we love.

One of the false arguments of those lovers of death and profit is that the "environmentalists" will take away jobs. Those who affirm life, then, are pitted against hearth and home, a man's ability to earn his dignity, his bread, his love, his children (sexism and patriarchy are part of the structure of this argument, an emotional linchpin in the turning of public opinion). Better a logger's job than a spotted owl, a little bird no one sees anyway (as though nature is a postcard or a zoo); better to feed a family than to be sentimental about the rings of a tree. Beyond the manipulation of our sense of community by the opportunism of the greedy, where does this cynical, duplicitous argument arise? Although I doubt that those who are using the arguments to their own purposes have motivations beyond the shallow base of their own bottom lines, when we listen to those arguments and are moved by them, I suggest it is at least in part due to the deep heritage we have been discussing here. We want to choose the logger over the owl because we are dualistic: we think of "civilization" as good and "wilderness" as evil; or we think of humans as the pinnacle of creation rather than a participant in this great experimental earth; or we think that by sentimentalizing subsistence labor, we will not have to examine the oppressive hierarchies of society.

Let's ask simply the first, easy question: why do logging jobs have to be preserved? Who speaks up for the wainwright, to stop Detroit and Japan, to keep roads paced for wagons? No one worries about the printing press taking jobs from scribes. Where are the hosiers and thimblemakers and parchment makers? Few of us are troubled that Mother Goose has been replaced by the television (although I suppose I am). In Genesis, all the ways of earning one's way in the world are divided up among those who are herders, those who are players upon the lyre and harp, and the forgers of metal, the sons of Jabal, Jubal, and Tubal-cain. What seems fundamental about human livelihood changes. In sixteenth-century illustrated catalogue celebrating crafts and tradespeople, there are two sorts of hunters, but there are no loggers. How many of us can get in the tub which fits a butcher, a baker, a candle-stick maker? Are well-meaning protectors of the livelihood of candle makers staging candlelight vigils against other forms of illumination?

To destroy an old-growth forest for ten years' of logging jobs makes the act of throwing the baby out with the bathwater superbly rational. If we are living through a night so cold that the children might freeze, will we pull down the house and burn it, with no thought to tomorrow? Will the children, without a house, freeze among the ashes of their short-sighted decision? All that seems to drive this argument for destruction of forests, of planet — are certainly not long-term economics, certainly not responsible communities nurturing families — is instead an ancient and unconscious mythic bias against the earth. The "boundaries" between civilization and the "savage" represent the limits of the minds who draw those lines. We must let our minds wander the forests. And the forests wander our mind. We breathe in concert, perhaps we dream in concert, too.

Of course we can log, or "harvest" forests and "clear" lands, we can use paper to sing to one another, but we need not destroy tomorrow, we need not act out the Western apocalyptic death wish. Loggers are also writers and readers, and we are after all, part of a mutual cycle of the use of trees. Sometimes I have to stop writing, when I forget the sacrifice, when I forget the paper underneath me. It is not necessary (and we must not let it be possible) that our grandchildren will lack not only paper and pencils but will lack air to breathe. Although no one should work for peanuts, I agreed to write this essay for a sack of filberts. My prayer is that we can share in eating the words, and give thanks to filbert trees.

Nature is an idea, not a given. Nature transforms to conform to a prevailing view of human nature. Nature is a perception, and perception is a construction. If we are to let the natural world tangle its own forests, sift its own deserts, lick its own young into shape, we will come to understand ourselves as part of that process, trust our own wilderness of mind. The way we think of nature is also nature. Our thoughts and our things are as natural as the sequoia. We can now risk seeing the sequoia, not as god, not as raw material, not as the demonic, not as a nothing in the way of something, but as a participant in the creation of consciousness. The mind of the tree affects the mind of the human.

Koko, the poetic gorilla who lives in Woodside, California can love a cat and name it Lips Lipstick; she is of the tribe of gorillas who have proven to us their capacities for language and love, and who may be extinguished. The elephant, the largest land mammal, may be doomed in our generation. What is the human mind without the mind of a gorilla, an elephant to remember us?

Whatever "nature" is, it is shaped by and shapes the human mind, like the mother bear's sculpting tongue, every time we adjust the environment, we adjust the mind. In the myth which is emerging now, we will love death, but also life. We have long been asking, "what do stars eat," and "are they animals?" They are reflected questions, questions about our own consciousness.

The Squirrel and the Telescope

by John Daniel

On a ten-thousand-foot mountaintop in southern Arizona, work has begun on a $200 million observatory that will aim three powerful new telescopes at the galaxies and nebulas of distant space. If some environmentalists have their way, the observatory won't be completed. Their concerns are closer to the ground than those of the scientists and institutions backing the project. Building the observatory will require the partial destruction of Mount Graham's old-growth forest of spruce and fir. That forest is a unique island ecosystem in a desert region; animal species don't migrate between Mount Graham and other mountain systems. One native animal, the Mount Graham red squirrel, is recognized as an endangered subspecies whose population probably numbers fewer than two hundred. With its forest habitat disrupted, the squirrel may very possibly be driven to extinction.

Such conflicts between the works of man and the existence of obscure animals have become almost commonplace since passage of the Endangered Species Act. Building a large dam imperils a species of small fish. A variety of butterfly stalls the development of an industrial park. For those of us who don't much believe in the need for more dams and industrial parks, the choice in such cases is usually clear — as clear as it is for those builders and boosters who dismiss our concerns as sentimental or as mere pretext for an antitechnology, antiprogress agenda. But the case of the observatory, for me, is more difficult. I don't know a lot about astronomy, but I find it exciting. I'm fascinated by the glimpses of the universe it reveals _ red giants and spiral nebulas, black holes and mysterious great walls in the far deeps of space and time. I would like to know more. A new industrial park is one more excess of our polluting growth economy. Most dams are built mainly to justify the federal agencies that build them. But a new observatory might tell us truths about the nature of the cosmos, and how it came to be, and how it might be evolving.

Should a tiny population of squirrels stand in the way? Secretary of the Interior Manuel Lujan, to his credit, has asked the question that must exist in many other minds: "Do we have to save every subspecies?" Obviously, the Mount Graham red squirrel could disappear from its place, and from the evolutionary life of Earth, and the life of no human being would change. The squirrels are so few in number that the ecosystem of the mountain itself would change only little. A niche would open, to be filled by other life forms, and the natural economy of the mountain would go on, altered but viable. Species have been dying out since the planet came to life, after all. Ninety-nine percent of all species ever to inhabit Earth are extinct.

But there's a distinction to be made. To equate the consciously destructive acts of *Homo sapiens* with the workings of evolution is to beg the question. Nature proceeds by its own unintentional genius, a genius that gives rise to the lives of individuals and species, and, in its own time, requires their deaths. We did not create the Mount Graham red squirrel and place it on its mountaintop, and so it is not for us to decide that the Mount Graham red squirrel is expendable. Three and a half billion years of evolutionary intelligence have gone into the squirrel's making, as into ours, as into all the interwoven lives of Earth. If we are capable of subjecting ourselves to anything, we should subject ourselves to that intelligence. We live, necessarily, by tampering with nature. We have tampered freely and destructively on this continent for five hundred years. It is time — past time — to hold ourselves and our tampering under careful limits.

But what of the observatory, and the window on the universe that it would open? I would like to know what it might show us. But interesting as that potential knowledge might be, the observatory in its present site epitomizes the tragic irony of our society's technical ambition and accomplishment. As our science sharpens its eyes, peering farther into remote space and deeper into the subatomic structure of matter, we see ourselves and our relationship to the rest of earthly nature with nothing close to sufficient clarity. The knowledge we most urgently need is the knowledge of how to act responsibly as a living member of Earth. Science has a major role to play in finding that knowledge, but nothing in the light of remote stars, or in the minute stirrings of quarks and gluons, is going to help us. The wisdom we need, if we find it at all, we'll find here, on the common surface of this homeland that gave birth to us, and to all the life we know.

CREDITS

John Callahan's sense of humor is shaped in part by a car accident which left him a quadriplegic in 1972. With David Kelly, he wrote his autobiography, *Don't Worry, He Won't Get Far on Foot*, and has two collection of cartoons, *Do Not Disturb Any Farther* and *Digesting the Child Within*. A third collection will be released fall 1992.

Kurt Caswell has written for *Northwest Parks and Wildlife*, *Northwest Travel*, and *Salt Lake City Magazine*, and worked as assistant editor at *Boise Magazine*. His fiction book *River Belly* will be published this year by cold-drill books. He is currently teaching English in Japan.

John Daniel is the poetry editor of *Wilderness* magazine. His poetry collection *Common Ground* was published by Confluence Press in 1988. Daniel's essays have appeared in numerous publications, including the *North American Review* and *Orion*. *The Trail Home*, his first book of prose, which includes "The Squirrel & the Telescope," will be published by Pantheon in June, 1992.

Nora Marks Dauenhauer & **Richard Dauenhauer** work at Sealaska Heritage Foundation in Juneau, Alaska to preserve native languages. Some of their books include *Haa Shuká, Our Ancestors: Tlingit Oral Narratives* and *Haa Tuwuuáagu Yís, for Healing Our Spirit: Tlingit Oratory*, both from University of Washington Press.

Barbara Drake teaches creative writing at Linfield College in McMinnville, Oregon. She is the author of two poetry collections: *What We Say to Strangers* from Breitenbush and *Bees in Wet Weather* from Canoe Press. In 1993 Harcourt, Brace & Jovanovich will publish a revised edition of her book *On Teaching Poetry*.

Tom Franks earned a Bachelor's in Philosophy and a Master's in Special and Early Childhood Education before deciding to become a freelance cartoonist. He has syndicated the editorial cartoon series "The Beaver State Advocate" to newspapers throughout Oregon since 1987.

Terry Glavin is the *Vancouver Sun's* native affairs reporter.

Jerome Gold, publisher of Black Heron Press, is the author of two novels, *The Inquisitor* and *The Negligance of Death*. He is working on a collection of interviews with Northwest book publishers and another novel.

Terri Lee Grell lives in Toutle, Washington, is the editor and publisher of Lynx, a quarterly journal of renga. Her work has been published in *Mirrors*, *Exquisite Corpse*,

Next Exit, Lost and Found Times, The Bellingham Review, and the anthology *Narrow Road to Renga.*

Christopher Harris' photographs are featured in *Beloved of Sky: Essays and Photographs on Clearcutting,* to be published in fall of 1992 by Broken Moon Press.

David Hedges has been writing for a living for 32 years and has written everything but audio-visuals. His short stories and poetry have been published in *The Christian Science Monitor, Samisdat, Northwest Magazine,* and *Calapooya Collage.*

Robert Heilman is a writer and storyteller in Myrtle Creek, Oregon. His articles have appeared in *The Oregonian, The Sun, The Table Rock Sentinel, The New Settler Interview,* and *The Siskyou Journal.* He is nearing completion of a book entitled *Manual Labor (and other things not taught in schools).*

Douglas Larsen is an adjunct professor in the Biology Department at Portland State University and also works independently as an environmental consultant and volunteer scientist. A limnologist (one who studies lakes), he has conducted research on lakes, reservoirs, rivers, and estuaries for the past 25 years in the Pacific Northwest.

Barry Lopez is the author of *Desert Notes, River Notes, Winter Court, Giving Birth to Thunder, Of Wolves and Men, Arctic Dreams, Crossing Open Ground,* and most recently, *Crow & Weasel.* His works have been translated into eleven languages, and *Arctic Dreams* won the National Book award in nonfiction.

Nancy Lord is the author of *Survival* (from Coffee House Press) and *The Compass Inside Ourselves: Short Stories* (from Fireweed Press). Her short story "Beluga" was chosen from 800 entries to be one of four winners of Sierra's 1991 nature-writing contest and published in the December issue. She fishes commercially in Alaska.

Jack McLarty's cover art "Ocumicho" was influenced by Mexican folk art themes. He taught printmaking and painting at the Pacific Northwest College of Art.

Richard Nelson is a cultural anthropologist who focuses on native peoples and their environments. His previous books include *Shadow of the Hunter, Hunters of the Northern Forest,* and *Make Prayers to the Raven,* which was developed into a PBS series narrated by Barry Lopez. His new book, *The Deer,* will be published by Knopf.

Paul Pintarich has worked at *The Oregonian* since 1965 and has been the book review editor since 1982. Novelist, poet, and essayist, Pintarich is currently writing an autobiographical account of how a craggy, middle-aged man endures the modern world.

Robert Pyle lives in the Willapa Hills of Washington. His book *Wintergreen: Listening to the Land's Heart* won the 1987 John Burroughs Medal for distinguished nature writing. Author of several books on butterflies, Pyle is currently compiling a book of Nabokov's butterfly writing. A book of essays and a novel are forthcoming.

David Quammen is the author of three novels including *The Soul of Viktor Tronko;* three novellas entitled *Blood Line: Stories of Fathers and Sons;* a collection of science essays *Natural Acts;* and is working on a new book to be published by William Morrow. He pens a column for *Outside* magazine.

Monty Reid, a native of Saskatchewan, has lived and worked in Alberta since 1968. He has authored seven books, including *The Life of Ryley, The Dream of Snowy Owls*, and *The Last Great Dinosaurs*, and was general editor of *A Nature Guide to Alberta*. Reid is assistant director of the Royal Museum of Paleontology in Drumheller.

Lynda Sexson teaches religious studies at Montana State University. She is the author of *Ordinarily Sacred*, and *Margaret of the Imperfections*. Lynda is working on a collection of stories and a novel.

Skanu'u (Ardythe Wilson) is a Gitksan researcher, speaker, and mother.

Susan Stanley is a journalist and writing instructor in Portland, Oregon. She is a frequent contributor to *Redbook, Family Circle*, and *Good Housekeeping*, among others. Stanley's book *Maternity Ward* is published by William Morrow.

David T. Suzuki, Professor of Zoology at the University of British Columbia, is the host of " The Nature of Things" and writes a syndicated weekly column. His books include science books for children and *Wisdom of the Elders: Honoring Sacred Native Concepts of Ecology* (with Peter Knudtson).

Sallie Tisdale lives in Oregon and is the author of *Sorcerer's Apprentice, Harvest Moon*, and *Lot's Wife*. She has had essays in *The New Yorker, Harper's, Esquire,* and other magazines.

Peter Douglas Ward is the author of *The Natural History of the Nautilus* and *In Search of Nautilus*. He is Professor of Geological Sciences and Curator of Invertebrates, Thomas Burke Museum at the University of Washington in Seattle.

Art Wilson is a Gitksan artist and lives in Hazelton, British Columbia.

William Woodall is a teacher, writer, and editor. He makes his home in Idaho, but currently teaches English in a South Korean university.

Fishtrap
P.O. Box 38
Enterprise, OR 97828

Workshops July 6-9
Fishtrap Gathering
July 10-12

Primus St. John   Jack Ohman
Sallie Tisdale   Daniel Kemmis
Primus St. John   Kim Stafford
Ed Marston   Rosalie Sorrels
Channa Taub   Alvin Josephy
Alan Siporin   Marc Jaffe
        Anne Taylor Fleming

PORTLAND STATE UNIVERSITY
SCHOOL OF EXTENDED STUDIES
SUMMER SESSION

Haystack

PROGRAM IN THE ARTS & SCIENCES

at Cannon Beach, Oregon

WRITING A FIRST NOVEL ■ MOLLY GLOSS
June 29 - July 3

VOICE OF THE SHORT STORY ■ SANDRA DORR
June 29 - July 3

WRITING FROM YOUR ROOTS ■ JUDITH BARRINGTON
July 6 - 10

HOLLYWOOD SCREENWRITING ■ MICHAEL HAUGE
July 11 & 12 (weekend workshop)

MYSTERY WRITING ■ M. K. WREN
July 13 - 17 or July 20 - 24

WRITING ESSAYS FOR RADIO ■ SCOTT SIMON
July 20 - 24

DANGEROUS WRITING ■ TOM SPANBAUER
July 20 - 24 or July 29 - August 2

NONFICTION STORYTELLING ■ JACK HART
July 27 - 31

PERSONAL POETRY: TRADITIONAL FORMS ■ TOM TRUSKY
July 27 - 31

FINDING AND FORMING FICTION ■ ANN COPELAND
August 3 - 7

FICTION WRITING TECHNIQUES ■ CRAIG LESLEY
August 3 - 7

*Registration is first come first served and
classes fill quickly. Call now for a brochure:
PSU Summer Session, (503) 725-4081.*

Natural Provocations from Pantheon

THE TRAIL HOME

Essays by
JOHN DANIEL

The prize-winning author of
Common Ground explores
ecological issues while he celebrates
mysteries that encompass and
surpass human existence. Elegant
and humorous, essays range
from the life of a packrat to
the existence of God.

*John Daniel is a winner of a Pushcart Prize
and a recipient of Stanford University's
Wallace Stegner Fellowship in Poetry.*

THE EAGLE BIRD
MAPPING A NEW WEST

CHARLES F. WILKINSON

One of the nation's preeminent experts on the law
of the American West explores the raging battle
for resources and the no longer clear-cut conflicts
between conservationists and developers.

**"The best handbook I know for
anyone who wants to know
the history of the West and its
probable future."**
— Wallace Stegner

"Smart, wise, wonderfully said."
— William Kittredge,
author of *A Hole in the Sky*

*Charles F. Wilkinson is Moses
Lasky Professor of Law at
the University of Colorado.*

At bookstores now or order directly by calling 1·800·733·3000   PANTHEON

THE NINEMILE WOLVES
AN ESSAY BY RICK BASS

Defiant and opinionated, Rick Bass has written an inspired essay advocating wolf reintroduction in the context of the fate of one small pack of wolves in northwest Montana. An environmental issue for all, philosophic for some and yet moral for Bass, the wolf and its return have in the past and again today polarized the West and ignited the passions of its inhabitants, whether cattle ranchers or environmental activists, wildlife biologists or hunters. The result of years of personal study and interviews with scores of people, both for and against reintroduction, *The Ninemile Wolves* is not so much scientific tract as one man's vigorous inquiry into the proper relationship between man and nature.

Cloth/$22.95

Other Titles from Clark City Press

Just Before Dark
by Jim Harrison/ cloth $24.95

A Good Man to Know
by Barry Gifford/ cloth $21.95

Death and the Good Life
by Richard Hugo/ paper $9.95

The Muddy Fork & Other Things
by James Crumley/ paper $12.95

And More
For current catalog and shipping charges, contact:

Clark City Press
POST OFFICE BOX 1358   LIVINGSTON, MONTANA 59047
(800) 835-0814   FAX (406) 222-3371
Distributed to the trade by Consortium (800) 283-3572

Free Gift for Poets

POET® MAGAZINE

is looking for
poets & writers
just like you

One of America's largest poetry publishers (hundreds of poems and articles published each year) is seeking poetry and how-to poetry articles from poets and writers at all levels of experience.

To request guidelines and your FREE informative and fun poetry publishing kit, please rush* three first class stamps with your request to

POET MAGAZINE
Free Poetry Publishing Kit
P.O. Box 54947, Dept. LB
Oklahoma City, OK 73154

*QUANTITIES LIMITED

"This is a wild and beautiful collection that I will keep close to me." —William Heyen

 **MOON CROSSING BRIDGE**
Poems by Tess Gallagher

GRAYWOLF PRESS / $17.00 cloth
2402 University Ave., Ste. 203, St. Paul, MN 55114
Distributed to the trade by Consortium (800) 283-3572

THE SPIRIT IN THE LAND
The worldview of the Gitksan & Wet'suwet'en
By Gisday Wa and Delgam Uukw
$14.00 ISBN 0-9692570-1-5

MOSS-HUNG TREES
Haiku of the West Coast, by Winona Baker
$10.00 ISBN 0-9692570-3-1

WILDWOOD: A FOREST FOR THE FUTURE
By Ruth Loomis with Merv Wilkinson
$10.00 ISBN 0-9692570-2-3

* * * * *

REFLECTIONS Publisher
P.O. Box 178
Gabriola, B.C. Canada V0R 1X0
(604) 247-8685

"A Prophet of Responsibility"

—Bill Kibben, *The New York Review of Books*

AMERICAN AUTHORS SERIES

Wendell Berry

In the first full-length study of Wendell Berry, editor Paul Merchant has assembled an unconventional volume that fits this unconventional man. New and unpublished work by Berry opens the volume. Essays by his contemporaries offer insights into the unique style of both a flawless stylist and combative polemicist. A gallery of photographs, plus the letters, poems and reminiscences of colleagues (including Wallace Stegner and Terry Tempest-Williams), reveal a personal side. This complete volume also offers an illuminating interview, a useful chronology of Berry's career, and an extensive bibliography of Berry's publications and of commentaries on his work.

Volume 4 of the Confluence American Authors Series; Paper $14.95, Cloth $24.95

Confluence Press, 8th Ave. & 6th St., Lewiston, ID 83501-2698 (208)799-2336

Writer's NW

the quarterly tabloid of the community of the printed word in the
Pacific Northwest
serving writers, readers, publishers, librarians, booksellers,
and teachers of writing, English, and journalism
with a windfall of news, reviews, essays, interviews, marketing
information, new book releases by NW presses and authors, and
the seductive Breviloquence Fiction Contests.

One-year subscriptions are only $10. Samples are $2.50.

Make checks payable in U.S. funds to
Blue Heron Publishing, Inc.
24450 NW Hansen Road
Hillsboro, Oregon 97124

To order by VISA or MC, phone 503/621-3911.

*O*RION

PEOPLE AND NATURE

**The Quarterly Magazine
of People and Nature**

*"Most nature magazines are beautiful because they are
full of color photographs....*Orion *is beautiful because
it is carefully designed to suit its purpose. And its
purpose is to present ideas related to the largest and
subtlest of themes."*

-Kevin McCarthy, The Bloomsbury Review

*"Hundreds of thousands of people all round the world
need to hear* Orion*'s message. Now that would make
a real difference!"*

-John Quinney, Seventh Generation

This internationally-acclaimed quarterly offers award-winning
articles, photography and art on a wide variety of topics.
Orion addresses the reconnection of human culture and the
human spirit with nature from the varied perspectives of
distinguished writers and conservationists.

With its Summer 1992 issue, *Orion* will be celebrating its 10th
anniversary. This special lengthier edition of the magazine will
include articles by Wendell Berry, John Elder, Joan Engel, John
Hay, Barry Lopez, Frederick Turner—plus celebratory images
by leading nature photographers.

Annual subscription-$16.00

ORION 136 East 64th Street New York, NY 10021
212-758-6475

LEFT BANK

A Northwest way to read between the lines — a potlatch of pointed prose and poetry.

Of #1, *Publishers Weekly* said,
> "The fishing pieces are uniformly excellent… The interviews with and homages to writers of the region…are useful and intelligently done.…"

Semiannual in December & June, **LEFT BANK** is a magazine in book form featuring NW writers on universal themes. Readers are treated to a provocative, entertaining, and evocative cross-section of creative nonfiction, fiction, essays, interviews, poetry, and art.

Themes and contributors are determined by an editorial staff and advisory board of respected writers, editors, and publishers representing Alaska, British Columbia, Idaho, Montana, Oregon, and Washington.

#1: Writing & Fishing the Northwest — this critically acclaimed first issue featured the likes of Wallace Stegner, Craig Lesley, Sharon Doubiago, Greg Bear, Nancy Lord, and John Keeble.

#2: Extinction — it's in your hands. Enjoy it before it disappears.

#3: Sex, Family, Tribe — it will surprise and delight and disturb you. Make room for it on your shelf. Order today.

CANADIAN BOOKSTORES ORDER FROM:
Milestone Publications Ltd.
P.O. Box 35548, Stn. E
Vancouver, B.C. V6M 4G8

U.S. BOOKSTORES ORDER FROM:
Consortium Book Sales & Dist.
287 East Sixth Street, Suite 365
St. Paul, Minnesota 55101

REQUEST OUR CATALOG. AND ASK FOR WRITERS' GUIDELINES — YOU JUST NEVER KNOW.